SURE
SALVATION

~~Timothy~~

May your assurance increase more and more.
1 Jn. 5:11,12!

~~Phil Mills~~

Also by Philip W. Dunham

Blinded by the Light

SURE
SALVATION

*You can **know** you have*
eternal life

PHILIP W.
DUNHAM

Pacific Press® Publishing Association
Nampa, Idaho
Oshawa, Ontario, Canada
www.pacificpress.com

Cover design by Michelle C. Petz
Inside design by Steve Lanto
Cover illustration © iStockphoto.com

The story of Dr. Robert Petterson related in chapter 15, "A Chosen Child," is excerpted from *The Day I Met God* © 2001 by Jim Covell, Karen Covell, and Victorya Michaels Rogers. Used by permission of Multnomah Publishers, Inc.

Unless otherwise noted, all Scripture quotations are from the Holy Bible, New King James Version, copyright © 1979, 1980, 1982 by Thomas Nelson, Inc. Used by permission.
Scripture quotations marked NIV are from the HOLY BIBLE, NEW INTERNATIONAL VERSION, copyright © 1973, 1978, 1984 International Bible Society. Used by permission of Zondervan Bible Publishers.
Scripture quotations marked NLT are taken from the Holy Bible, New Living Translation, copyright © 1996. Used by permission of Tyndale House Publishers, Inc., Wheaton, Illinois 60189. All rights reserved.
Scripture quotations marked TLB are from *The Living Bible*, Paraphrased, copyright © 1971 by Tyndale House Publishers, Wheaton, Ill. Used by permission.
Scripture quotations marked *The Message* are copyright © 1993 by Eugene H. Peterson. Used by permission of NavPress Publishing Group.
Scripture quotations attributed to the Contemporary English Version are copyright © American Bible Society 1991, 1995. Used by permission.
Scripture quotations attributed to J. B. Phillips are from *The New Testament in Modern English*, Revised Edition, copyright © J. B. Phillips 1958, 1960, 1972. Used by permission of Macmillan Publishing Co., Inc.
Scripture quotations attributed to *The New English Bible* are copyright © The Delegates of the Oxford University Press and the Syndics of the Cambridge University Press 1961, 1970.
Scripture quotations marked NCV are from *The Everyday Bible, New Century Version*, copyright © 1987, 1988 by Word Publishing, Dallas, Texas 75039. Used by permission.

ISBN 13: 978-0-8163-2178-0
ISBN 10: 0-8163-2178-7

Additional copies of this book are available by calling toll-free 1-800-765-6955 or by visiting http://www.adventistbookcenter.com.

07 08 09 10 11 • 5 4 3 2 1

This book is dedicated to

our son and his wife, Dennis and Jami Dunham,

our daughter and her husband, Diane and Tom Eyserbeck,

and our grandchildren and great-grandchildren

with the fervent hope and prayer that each of us

will possess not only the joy but the assurance of salvation

and spend eternity together as a family.

Contents

Preface

"Jesus loves me! This I know, for the Bible tells me so." Cradle roll stuff, right? Isn't it interesting that children seem to have no problem with this universe-shaking idea and all that it implies? They sing it. They shout it. And can you imagine?—they just believe the whole song for what it says, as if it were true or something!

But a problem arises for many of us adult cradle rollers because this hymn that is so well-known and well-loved by children goes on to say, "Little ones to Him *belong,*" as in "I am His and He is mine," "I'm a part of His family," "He is my Brother." And while we may accept the rather wonderfully generic "Jesus loves me" part, the "little ones to Him belong" aspect suggests such a foreign belongingness, such an almost presumptive assurance, such a matter-of-fact acceptance, that some of us find it hard to apply it to ourselves personally.

Why is this so? Let me count the ways.

- "Because I'm not worthy."
- "Because I'm not good enough."
- "Because of all the wrong things I've done—some even quite recently."
- "Because I fall much too often."
- "Because I *know* much more than I *do.*"

- "Because He certainly could love *others,* and *they* could belong to Him, but I'm me, and . . ."
- "Because the Bible says, 'We know that whoever is born of God does not sin,' but I sin."
- And "because, because, because . . ."

As Ellen White exclaimed, "How many, by their actions, if not in word, are saying, 'The Lord does not mean this for me. Perhaps He loves others, but He does not love me.' "[1]

Now, suppose we created a stanza for this song that went like this: "Jesus *saves* me! This I know, for the Bible tells me so." The children wouldn't have any problem with this version of the song. They would still sing and shout it. They're not yet old enough and smart enough to doubt. But among adults, the ranks of the doubters would likely swell to many, many more. There would be all of the "becauses" above plus a splendid new assortment, because a stanza like that contains just too much assurance.

My many years of contact and conversation with my fellow Seventh-day Adventists lead me to believe that many of them might sincerely claim as their theme song "Is My Name Written There?" ("I wonder, I wonder, I wonder. I doubt that it is. I hope so, but slim chance.") To the honor and glory and delight of God, the theme song of every Seventh-day Adventist Christian should be "When the Roll Is Called Up Yonder, I'll Be There."

The purpose of this book is not to comfort the sinners in Zion nor to give license to Laodicean living, nor to wink at or excuse known sin, nor to promote "sin-and-live theology." God forbid! Rather, I wish to help us revel in the delicious assurance that every true believer can have, *should have,* in the " 'Lamb of God who takes away the sin of the world!' " (John 1:29).

---

1. Ellen G. White, *Steps to Christ* (Mountain View, Calif.: Pacific Press®, 1956), 18.

CHAPTER 1

My Journey Toward Assurance

I was seventeen, very worldly, and totally absorbed in "doing what comes naturally," which meant pleasure, excitement, fun, diversion, and virtually anything unspiritual. My mom would ask me to go to church with her on Sabbath, but Saturday was a poker, smoking, drinking, mess-around day, and I was just too busy and very not interested.

My brother was in the Navy Air Corps at that time. Like countless other fellows, he loved a girl back home. He sent me money to take her out to shows and dances to "keep her in the family"—a real "brotherly trust" thing to do.

Then my brother became a Seventh-day Adventist Christian while still in the service. A short while later, his girlfriend found the same life-changing experience with Christ. Both of them, especially my brother, witnessed to me in an appropriate, tactful manner and arranged for me to be given a copy of Ellen White's book *Steps to Christ.*

While reading that book, I came under deep conviction regarding my sins, lostness, and estrangement from God. Rather late one evening, I was walking home after having gone to a theater. Somehow, the Spirit of God touched me so strongly that when I got home, I knelt down sobbing, confessed my sins, and cried out to God to save a young "wretch" like me.

My life changed drastically. Knowing when one was converted isn't necessarily essential to being truly converted, but I surely know when I gave my heart to the Lord and became a Christian. God gave me great peace, joy, and victory. And everything changed: Overnight, I was newly born in Christ, and the sins of the flesh dropped away. My friends changed; my habits changed; my tastes changed; my language changed; my pleasures changed; and my goals changed. The neighbor lady, observing that I was actually home and helping around in the yard, asked my mom, "What happened to Phil?"

My brother's girlfriend and I were baptized into Christ and the Seventh-day Adventist faith on the same Sabbath in the old Grand River Church in Detroit, Michigan, by Pastor N. R. Dower. We were baptized in March, and by the end of August, I had enrolled as a senior in La Sierra Preparatory School in Riverside, California (which became La Sierra Academy a year or two later). Shortly after my conversion, I had chosen to become a doctor, but a few months into that senior year, God gave me a definite call to the ministry. Four years and a wife and newborn son later, I finished college and was called into the Southeastern California Conference as a ministerial intern.

This is hard to share, but in my early years as a Christian and even halfway into my ministry, my focus was more on duty, obedience, "truth," performance, correctness, behavior, sanctification, and crossing the t's and dotting the i's, and less on the real and beautiful simplicity of the gospel and the precious Savior Himself. I didn't exclude Jesus, but I saw Him as primarily my Helper in achieving all that He had achieved.

Yes, I preached about Jesus. Yes, I made altar calls for people to accept Him as their personal Savior. Yes, I would have acknowledged that faith in Him was more important than faith in doctrines. However, my emphasis was more on the one and only true church than on the one and only Christ. And perhaps I could relate too well to a pastor who was described as "a loud and angry man who spent too much of his time conjuring up new sins."

My tendency was to preach more on the first half of the Laodicean message, Revelation 3:15–17—the lukewarmness, the "wretched, miserable, poor, blind, and naked" part—rather than on verses 18–21, which Ellen White described as "filled with encouragement." During those too many years, if I had been confronted (and I was at times) by a good Baptist who asked, "Are you saved?" I would have been rather uncomfortable. My answer would have ranged from one that was vague to one that was circuitous, with something of a "hope so" aura. Did we not, in fact, have counsel that we should not say that we are saved?

In those years, I experienced ups and downs—wide swings in my feelings of salvation. My happiness was quite dependent on how I was doing at that particular moment. I also had a proclivity toward judging people based on whether or not they had overcome on the points I had overcome, even if my overcoming had occurred just recently. I considered it a simple matter of fact that everyone ought to have reached the high state of sanctification that I had reached.

A defining moment

One day, I received a call from Ken Livesay—at the time, the lay activities director of the Southeastern California Conference. He suggested that I join several other pastors in attending a weeklong seminar at the Campus Crusade for Christ headquarters at Arrowhead Springs, in San Bernardino, California. The seminar was on how to share the gospel and lead people to Jesus Christ.

My reaction to my wife was whiny and a bit petulant, with a delicious flavor of wounded self-righteousness. "Why should I go?" I asked. "There's no need. What more could they share than we already know as Seventh-day Adventists? Don't we have more light than they have?" I just didn't want to go. However, after more considered thought, I felt that I should at least accommodate my friend who had kindly asked me.

The people I met were wholesome and sincere. They didn't know some of the truths of the Bible that I knew, but they knew Christ and were intent on sharing Him with as many people as they could reach; they gave a centrality to Jesus that warmed my heart. Some of the major spiritual presentations were "How to Live the Cleansed Life," "How to Love by Faith," "How to Be Filled With the Spirit," and "How to Fulfill the Great Gospel Commission." Over and over again, they uplifted Jesus with such beauty and simplicity that my soul was mightily stirred.

One of the subjects that moved me strongly was "How to Be Filled With the Spirit."

The presenter spoke on Ephesians 5:18, where Paul wrote, "Be not drunk with wine, wherein is excess; but be filled with the Spirit" (KJV). He then added that the expression "be filled with the Spirit" is both a command and a promise.

The whole concept of living a Spirit-filled life really captured my longing. I drove home that evening anxious to get into my study to check out Ephesians 5:18 more closely, and, as a good Adventist pastor, to see what Ellen White had to say about this text. I was directed in my search to a statement in the book *Thoughts From the Mount of Blessing:* "To Jesus, who emptied Himself for the salvation of lost humanity, the Holy Spirit was given without measure. So it will be given to every follower of Christ when the whole heart is surrendered for His indwelling. Our Lord Himself has given the *command,* 'Be filled with the Spirit' (Ephesians 5:18), and *this command is also a promise* of its fulfillment."[1]

Praise God! Had the presenter read this book or something?

Toward the close of the week, the leaders of the program introduced us to a hymn that I had never before heard: "Like a River Glorious." This hymn seemed to capture and seal the blessing of assurance, peace, and rest that I had found during that special week. Here are the words:

Like a river glorious Is God's perfect peace,
Over all victorious In its bright increase;
Perfect, yet it floweth Fuller every day,
Perfect, yet it groweth Deeper all the way.

Hidden in the hollow Of His blessed hand,
Never foe can follow, Never traitor stand;
Not a surge of worry, Not a shade of care,
Not a blast of hurry Touch the spirit there.

Every joy or testing Comes from God above,
Given to His children As an act of love;
We may trust Him fully All for us to do—
Those who trust Him wholly Find Him wholly true.

Chorus:
Trusting in Jehovah, Hearts are fully blest—
Finding, as He promised, Perfect peace and rest.[2]

When I returned home from that week, I had changed. In a way, I had changed as much as I had at the time of my conversion in high school. When I shared with my wife the blessings I had newly experienced in Christ, she said she wanted them too. Later, we had the opportunity to go together to the same seminar, and she did find what I had found—*whom* I had found.

Then, following my sermons, members of my congregation in Arlington, California—which at the time numbered a thousand, meeting in two services—began to make comments, the gist of which was "Pastor, we don't know what has happened to you, but keep it up." My life had changed. My preaching had changed. And then my work changed, for I was asked to conduct seminars all over southeastern California, and subsequently in other fields as well, on how to share Christ and the gospel.

Four very important points: (1) I'm not saying I couldn't have found this concept of assurance, in time, from some of the "gospel giants" within the Adventist Church. Others have. I happened to have found it elsewhere. (2) I didn't become a Methodist Adventist or an Episcopalian Adventist. I did become a more Christ-centered Adventist pastor. (3) I didn't believe less in the unique nature and calling of the Seventh-day Adventist movement, but I did believe more and see more clearly the sweet simplicity of the gospel. (4) I didn't preach less about the commandments, the Sabbath, and the distinguishing points of the faith that God has revealed to this people, but I did preach more about Jesus, the gospel, the assurance we can have in Jesus, and righteousness by faith. And in the years following, "the longer I serve Him, the sweeter He grows." I want to share that experience with you.

---

1. Ellen G. White, *Thoughts From the Mount of Blessing* (Nampa, Idaho: Pacific Press®, 1956), 21; emphasis added.

2. Hymn # 74 in the *Seventh-day Adventist Hymnal* (Hagerstown, Md.: Review and Herald®, 1985).

CHAPTER 2

Eternal Security vs. Infernal Insecurity

It was a very difficult delivery that evening at Castle Memorial Hospital on the windward side of Oahu. The lives of both mother and baby teetered on the edge, and Dr. Bob Chung and Dwayne, a male nurse in attendance, did everything they could with their God-given professional skills to snatch life from the jaws of death. After intense, focused, stressful, prayer-filled moments, the welcome cries of the baby signaled life, and the mother's life was no longer in doubt. Sweat was wiped from foreheads. Tensions eased. The crisis was past.

Dr. Chung was a man of many interests and skills—among them, flying. After the tedious medical procedure, he suggested to Dwayne that they take a spin in his twin-engine, six-passenger Bonanza and relax a little by looking at the shimmering lights of Honolulu from the night sky—an unforgettable sight. "See if your wife and some of your children would like to go along too," he invited. Alice and two of the children decided not to go, but Dwayne's two other children and his aunt and uncle, who were visiting from the mainland, felt the flight would be exciting.

Soon, they arrived at Honolulu International Airport. The plane was readied, all six of them climbed in and buckled their seat belts, the engines roared to life, and Dr. Bob taxied from the tarmac onto the runway. Moments later, the tower cleared him for takeoff, and he nursed the powerful plane into the night air. Then, to the delighted gaze of the plane's occupants, there spread out before them the fairyland sights of this "paradise of the Pacific" at nighttime. It must have been memorable. But it wasn't to be long in the memories of the ill-fated six.

They were descending toward the airport, approaching the H1 freeway at a low altitude, when something went horribly wrong. Evidently, one of the engines failed, for the plane spiraled uncontrollably into the ground in a fiery crash just short of the busy freeway. All six occupants died instantly. Of course, the tragedy forever blighted the lives of their families and friends. But because Dr. Chung was the police commissioner of Honolulu and a well-known island business executive as well as a doctor, it also affected the lives of people across the entire state.

I lived in Hawaii at that time, and I drove by the charred wreckage a number of times on my way to and from the airport. Each time, my heart was sickened at the tragic, sudden ending of the lives of six of God's children. And I couldn't help but be forced to think that at the time of their death, their probation was closed; their cases were forever decided. They were either saved or lost. Most Christians wouldn't question this fact.

Then another thought exploded in my mind. If those people were either saved or lost at the moment of impact, what about five minutes before the crash? What about five hours, or five days, or five weeks, or five months, or five years before that moment of finality? It began to dawn upon me as never before that at every moment of every day, we are either saved or lost. As professing Christians, we live in a constant state of either/or.

This can be a very unsettling thought. Why? Because so many of us are inclined to think of ourselves as kind of, sort of, maybe, perhaps, somewhere in between saved or lost. We tend to think there has to be a little latitude; there must be a third option. We think the "saved or lost" concept is too rigid, too uncomfortable—the reason being that we're not quite good enough to be saved and not quite bad enough to be lost, so all we're left with is a dangling uncertainty about our present salvation.

As we process these thoughts, we may be led to one or the other of two extremes—two ditches, if you please. One is known as eternal security. The other I wish to refer to as infernal insecurity. The first is a cardinal teaching of our friends the Baptists and others. The second is a condition in which too many Seventh-day Adventists find themselves. We need to examine both of these extremes.

The eternal security ditch

On the one hand, we have eternal security—the belief that has come to be known popularly as "once saved, always saved." You couldn't find either of these terms in a theological handbook. However, they describe in essence the deeply and widely held belief that if you have truly believed in Christ as your personal Savior, and if you have truly confessed and repented of your sins, then you are truly saved, and nothing—not anything—can change that.

The key word here is *truly,* because if you should somehow fall away into sin and apostasy, then you were not *truly* saved in the first place. At least, that's how those who believe in eternal security deal with the many texts in the Bible that speak of the apostasy of believers. In other words, people who apostatize didn't truly believe, didn't truly confess, and didn't truly repent to begin with. If they had, they couldn't have fallen away from their saved position.

I don't think this is a deliberate attempt to provide a "sinning license." But abused, this doctrine can create a false sense of assurance that in practice says that lifestyle doesn't matter, open sin doesn't matter, living as the world lives doesn't matter. People rationalize, "I was truly converted once: I believed, repented, confessed my sins, and received Christ. So that means I am still truly saved now, no matter how my life might appear at the moment." My portrayal of this attitude is not a matter of conjecture; it's a matter of fact. I've had firsthand experience with people who really believe this way, and who act on their belief.

To counter the above problem, the church that most prominently advocates "once saved, always saved" also puts forward the doctrine of "final perseverance." The idea is that grace in the heart will produce perseverance in Christian growth to the end. So if you take advantage of the cardinal teaching of eternal security and feel sinning doesn't make any difference and you don't persevere in bearing the fruit of the Spirit, you weren't properly "graced" in the first place. In other words, "final perseverance" is a rather circular type of theology intended to protect the original thesis of "once saved, always saved."

The problem is that a perfect Lucifer became a perfect devil. The problem is that Adam and Eve were *truly* in the image of God, holy, righteous, and sinless—but the terrible reality is that they fell away. Then there's the case of King Saul. Scripture has the prophet Samuel telling the newly anointed king, " 'Then the Spirit of the LORD will come upon you, and you will prophesy with them *and be turned into another man' "* (1 Samuel 10:6, emphasis added). Verse 9 of the same chapter says, "And so it was, when he had turned his back to go from Samuel, *that God gave him another heart"* (emphasis added).

These Old Testament phrases could have come right out of the New Testament lexicon of born-again theology. King Saul was truly changed. But, sadly, he truly turned away from the Lord. His fall from grace was so dramatic and so evident that 1 Samuel 28:6 says, "When Saul inquired of the LORD, the LORD did not answer him, either by dreams or by Urim or by the prophets." Saul himself recognized the unspiritual pit that he had dug for himself. He said, " 'God has departed from me and does not answer me anymore' " (1 Samuel 28:15). Saul's last two tragic acts were inquiring of a medium, which God forbade and condemned, and committing suicide.

First Chronicles 10:13 contains Saul's epitaph: "Saul died for his unfaithfulness which he had committed against the LORD, because he did not keep the word of the LORD, and also because he consulted a medium for guidance." So, Saul went from truly saved to truly lost.

The infernal insecurity ditch

At the opposite extreme from eternal security is the state of so many good, sincere, conscientious, earnest Seventh-day Adventists. It's the one that I have already alluded to as infernal insecurity. Adventists know so much of the Bible. They enjoy so much light. They have a knowledge of the prophecies that exceeds that of most members and even pastors of other churches. They have an additional body of inspiration that verifies and enhances the Scripture. They are very focused on behavior and lifestyle issues. They exalt the law of God. They know that we are living in the end times. They know and believe so much that is right. But for so many dear believers, instead of a "blessed assurance," there is a cloud of "miserable misgivings." This cloud eclipses the sunshine, the joy, the certainty, and the assurance of their salvation in Christ that every trusting believer can and should have. This is an unresolved problem for so many; they are in an unsettled, relational limbo in their Christian life.

If someone were to confront these unsure individuals with the question "Are you saved?" they most likely would be nonplused, uncomfortable, and hesitating. And if someone were to approach them with the question "If Christ came today or if you died tonight, would you be ready to meet Him?" they would be in a similar quandary of uncertainty and discomfort. In either case, they would be uncomfortable because they're unsure of their current state of salvation.

I have asked the latter two questions in dozens of Adventist homes, and very few members were able to give an unqualified Yes. We have been schooled in uncertainty over the years. Our focus has so often been inward rather than upward, on ourselves first instead of Jesus first. The reasons for this are many. We will mention them as we continue to examine this issue of assurance and how much confidence in our salvation we can have without crossing over into the never-never land of presumption.

Whatever thoughts might be co-mingling in your head right now, please try to remember that when the plane crashed just short of the Honolulu International Airport, the five passengers and the pilot were either saved or lost. We're not speaking of degrees of justification or sanctification or a state of character perfection or anything else. The big question is, were they in a saving relationship with Jesus Christ? Again, please remember that while the circumstances might be different for each of us, the big question is the same. *And there is an answer!* Martin Luther knew the answer. He said, "When I look at myself, I don't see how I can ever be saved. When I look at Jesus, I don't see how I can ever be lost."

As Seventh-day Adventist Christians, we have to make certain that our witness is not, "Why don't you come and join our church, and then you can be as miserably uncertain of your salvation as we are." Further, we must learn that it is not "blessed unbelief" or "blessed uncertainty" or "blessed misgivings," but rather "blessed assurance, Jesus is mine."

CHAPTER 3

The Simplicity of Salvation

Which would you prefer to struggle with: 2 + 2 = 4 or $E = mc^2$ (which is Einstein's theory of relativity)? Salvation has to be simple enough for a child to understand. It has to be simple enough for the 2.5 billion people in the world who are illiterate and may be introduced to Christ only through a picture roll. And if the invitation "*Whoever desires,* let him take the water of life freely" (Revelation 22:17, emphasis added) truly applies to everyone—anyone on the planet at any time—then salvation has to be simple enough to be heard, understood, received, and acted upon. So you can make salvation as complicated as you wish, but please remember that it has to be simple enough.

Or do you really have a grasp of soteriology and soteriological terminology such as *justification, sanctification, regeneration, forensic righteousness, extrinsic righteousness, predestination,* and *election?* Schleiermacher elects all men subjectively, Lutherans all men objectively, Arminians all believers, and Augustinians all foreknown as God's own. Regarding the application of redemption, Martineau says that simultaneity doesn't exclude duration since each cause has duration and each effect also has duration. Right?

Talk about theological jargon!

Then there is John 3:16: " 'For God so loved the world that He gave His only begotten Son, that *whoever* believes in Him should not perish but have everlasting life,' " (emphasis added). It isn't too complicated, is it? One sentence. Twenty-five words. You can repeat it in ten seconds. If you were a primary child repeating it on Thirteenth Sabbath in front of the adult Sabbath School, you might be able to repeat it in five seconds. Furthermore, you can even understand what Jesus is saying.

One pastor had six hundred sermon outlines on John 3:16. Amazing! And if that wasn't impressive enough, he made a very bold statement about this text: "If all the Bible were destroyed except John 3:16, anyone, anywhere could be saved by believing this oft-quoted and cherished verse."

Did this pastor have an unbalanced emphasis on the love of God, the character of God? I don't think so. Ellen White pointed out, "Christ's favorite theme was the paternal character and abundant love of God."[1] More than this, in the book *Testimonies to Ministers,* she refers to the conversation Christ had with Nicodemus. Then she quoted John 3:16 and stated, "This lesson is one of the greatest importance to every soul that lives; *for the terms of salvation are here laid out in distinct lines. If one had no other text in the Bible, this alone would be a guide for the soul.*"[2]

To me, this means that if our Bible were composed of two covers with one page inside, and on the middle of that page it had one text, John 3:16, we'd have enough for salvation! Can we take that in? Or is it so simple that we aren't getting it? John 3:16 contains "the terms of salvation."

Even less complicated

Let's try to make this still less complicated. *The Desire of Ages* says, "It is when Christ is received as a personal Saviour that *salvation comes to the soul.*"[3]

This is soul boggling! Can it be? Is it really true? Is receiving salvation this simple? Is there an illustration to help us grasp this?

There is.

Luke 23:42, 43 records an incredible, twenty-two word exchange (depending on which Bible version you use) between a dying thief and a dying Savior. " 'Lord, remember me when You come into Your king-dom.' . . . 'Assuredly I say to you, today you will be with Me in Para-dise.' " Does this mean that the thief found salvation that quickly? Went from lost to saved that fast? Do you mean that salvation took only about ten seconds? Are we looking at a sinner becoming a saint with only a two-sentence Bible study and not the entire forty lessons?

The story of the thief finding salvation is that simple and that fast. He saw himself. He saw Jesus. He asked Him if he could be in heaven with Him. And Jesus said Yes. As a friend of mine says about some-thing exceptionally great, "How do you like them apples?"

The Story of Redemption says, "In Jesus, bruised, mocked, and hang-ing upon the cross, he saw his Redeemer, his only hope, and appealed to Him in humble faith."[4] So, in this ten-second exchange, the thief went from lost to saved, from raunchy to redeemed, from a perfect mess to a perfect man, from lawbreaker to law keeper, from son of the devil to son of the living God, from 100 percent wickedness to 100 percent righteousness, from sinner to saint, from hell and eternal dam-nation to heaven and eternal salvation.

Someone will ask, "What about character perfection?" Was the thief anything but a perfect thief? How do you go from perfect flop to just plain perfect in such a short time? Jesus said, " 'Be perfect' " (Matthew 5:48). Did the thief reach that in the blink of an eye?

There are many things I don't know, but I do know what *Steps to Christ* says. "If you give yourself to Him, and then accept Him as your Saviour, then, sinful as your life may have been, for His sake you are accounted righteous. Christ's character stands in place of your charac-ter, *and you are accepted before God just as if you had not sinned.*"[5] Long-time Christians who have a problem with assurance need to remember that we are looking at salvation at its irreducible minimum. We are looking at bottom-line salvation. Beginners' salvation.

This is so important.

- Salvation is a gift—Ephesians 2:8.
- Christ Himself is a gift—2 Corinthians 9:15.

- Justification is a gift—Romans 5:15–19.
- Sanctification is a gift—1 Corinthians 1:30.
- Repentance is a gift—Acts 5:31.
- Faith is a gift—Romans 12:3.
- The Holy Spirit is a gift—Acts 2:38.
- Grace is a gift—Ephesians 2:8.
- Forgiveness is a gift—Acts 5:31.
- Victory over sin is a gift—1 Corinthians 15:57.
- A new heart is a gift—Ezekiel 36:26.
- Righteousness is a gift—Romans 5:17.
- Eternal life is a gift—Romans 6:23.

It is actually rather simple to receive a gift. My wife, Evie, and I were given a car as a college graduation gift. We had been married for two years at the time, and our mode of transportation was a bicycle. Not a new one by any means, and it wasn't a Schwinn. The promise of a car from my parents and my aunt was almost too much for us to take in. But we were indeed taking it in and counting on the promise.

The graduation was at hand. The night came for us to go over to my parents' house to pick up the car. Ordinarily, we really liked to visit with them, but that night something was making us want the visit to end. Finally, after seven or eight hours of visiting, or so it seemed, my dad excused himself, went into his study, and came back out with the car's title transfer paper. He extended the keys and the paper, and I merely reached out and took what he offered me. Unbelievable but true. Easiest way we ever acquired a car. Simple!

When it comes to receiving the gifts of God, the process is especially simple because all the gifts come wrapped up in one beautiful, matchless package—Jesus Christ. So, go ahead—snow me with your latest scholarly insights into Pauline theology. Overpower me with your theological vocabulary. Make me feel small with your grasp of the cosmological, teleological, anthropological, and ontological arguments about the existence of God. But just don't confuse me, OK? Don't get me off the main track.

John 1:12 is pretty simple: "As many as received Him, to them He gave the right to become children of God, to those who believe in His name."

First John 5:11, 12 is pretty simple: "And this is the testimony: that God has given us eternal life, and this life is in His Son. He who has the Son has life; he who does not have the Son of God does not have life."

You see, I'm a great sinner. That's simple.

Jesus is a great Savior. That's simple.

If I ask Him, as the thief did, to be my Savior and give me His salvation and to remember me in His kingdom, He will. That's simple too.

Beautifully simple salvation

Salvation is simply beautiful and beautifully simple. Many of us, however, have this innate ability to make it complicated, cumbersome, and wearying.

The thief found righteousness by faith. The thief found sanctification by faith. The thief found perfection by faith. The thief found sinlessness by faith. The thief found completeness by faith. The thief found salvation by faith.

When you have Jesus by faith, then you have *everything* by faith. You have all that He was and all that He did by faith. Then, when God looks at you, all He sees is Jesus, His Son.

" 'Lord, remember me when You come into Your kingdom.' . . . 'Assuredly, I say to you, today you will be with Me in Paradise.' "

I want what the thief found. I want *whom* the thief found. I want to turn to Jesus, the Lamb of God who takes away the sin of the world, in total helplessness, dependence, and trust, as the thief did. I want to rejoice and revel in the beauty and simplicity of salvation as a Christian can and should. And it is as simple as John 3:16 and this simple story.

In the city of Chicago one cold, dark night, a blizzard was setting in. A little boy was selling newspapers on the corner as the people were going in and out of the cold. The little boy was so cold that he wasn't trying to sell many papers.

He walked up to a policeman and said, "Mister, you wouldn't happen to know where a poor boy could find a warm place to sleep tonight would you? You see, I sleep in a box up around the corner there and down the alley, and it's awful cold in there tonight. Sure would be nice to have a warm place to stay."

The policeman looked down at the little boy and said, "You go down the street to that big white house, and you knock on the door. When they come to the door, you just say John 3:16, and they'll let you in."

So he did. He walked up the steps and knocked on the door, and a lady answered. He looked up and said, "John 3:16." The lady said, "Come on in, son." She took him in and she sat him down in a split-bottom rocker in front of a great big old fireplace, and she went off. The boy sat there for a while and thought to himself, *John 3:16. . . . I don't understand it, but it sure makes a cold boy warm.*

Later she came back and asked him, "Are you hungry?" He said, "Well, just a little. I haven't eaten in a couple of days, and I guess I could stand a little bit of food." The lady took him in the kitchen and sat him down to a table full of wonderful food. He ate and ate until he couldn't eat any more. Then he thought to himself, *John 3:16. . . . Boy, I don't understand it, but it sure makes a hungry boy full.*

She took him upstairs to a bathroom, to a huge bathtub filled with warm water, and he sat there and soaked for a while. As he soaked, he thought to himself, *John 3:16. . . . I don't understand it, but it sure makes a dirty boy clean. . . .*

The lady came in and got him. She took him to a room, tucked him into a big old feather bed, pulled the covers up around his neck, kissed him goodnight, and turned out the lights. As he lay in the darkness and looked out the window at the snow coming down on that cold night, he thought to himself, *John 3:16. . . . I don't understand it, but it sure makes a tired boy rested.*

The next morning the lady came back up and took him down again to that same big table full of food. After he ate, she took him back to that same big old split-bottom rocker in front of the fireplace and picked up a big old Bible. She sat down in front of him and looked into his young face. "Do you understand John 3:16?" she asked gently. He replied, "No, ma'am, I don't. The first time I ever heard it was last night when the policeman told me to say it."

She opened the Bible to John 3:16 and began to explain to him about Jesus. Right there, in front of that big old fireplace, he gave his heart and life to Jesus. He sat there and thought, *John 3:16. . . . I don't understand it, but it sure makes a lost boy feel safe.*

You know, I have to confess that I don't understand it either—how God was willing to send His Son to die for me, and how Jesus would agree to do such a thing. I don't understand the agony of the Father and every angel in heaven as they watched Jesus suffer and die. I don't understand the intense love for *me* that kept Jesus on the cross till the end. I don't understand it, but it sure does make life worth living.[6]

1. Ellen G. White, *Testimonies for the Church* (Nampa, Idaho: Pacific Press®, 1948), 6:55.

2. White, *Testimonies to Ministers and Gospel Workers* (Nampa, Idaho: Pacific Press®, 1944), 370; emphasis added.

3. White, *The Desire of Ages* (Nampa, Idaho: Pacific Press®, 1940), 556; emphasis added.

4. White, *The Story of Redemption* (Hagerstown, Md.: Review and Herald®, 1949), 223.

5. White, *Steps to Christ* (Hagerstown, Md.: Review and Herald®, 1956), 42; emphasis added.

6. Author unknown.

CHAPTER 4

There Has to Be a Way

There just has to be a way to make it into the kingdom, into heaven itself, into the very presence of God forever and ever. And while I may not know myself—my own heart—as well as I should, I know for sure that *I am not the way*. I know that because I know what I am. I know what I am naturally, apart from God. The Word of God spells it out all too clearly, too pointedly.

Romans 3:10 says, "As it is written: 'There is none righteous, no, not one.'" The Contemporary English Version says, "No one is acceptable to God!" The GOD'S WORD Translation puts it like this, "Not one person has God's approval." I think I get it.

Romans 3:23 is also terribly inclusive when it reads, *"All* have sinned and come short of the glory of God" (KJV; emphasis added). Hmm. I think this means me.

Apart from God, I'm guilty as sin. In fact, I'm a classic example of total depravity. I'm a fountain of corruption. I am Mr. Mess-Up of the twenty-first century. On my own, as far as salvation is concerned, I am a disaster—not one that's waiting to happen, one that's already happened. I'm a flaming crash, a brick-wall collision at one hundred miles an hour. I have as much chance of getting to heaven on my own as I do of broad jumping the Grand Canyon.

Sure, I have some brains, a measure of intelligence. Of course, I do some good things at times; some polite things; occasionally, some things that may even look great. However, when it comes to deserving heaven, I'm essentially morally and spiritually bankrupt.

This is the very hard part. Knowing what I really am apart from God is one thing. But then, coming to realize what I ought to be . . . this really widens the Grand Canyon. And I have to face it, as do we all.

- Jesus said very pointedly, " 'Therefore . . . be perfect, just as your Father in heaven is perfect' " (Matthew 5:48). Could He really have meant this?
- Ephesians 5:27 tells us exactly what we ought to be and what Christ wants—"a glorious church, not having spot or wrinkle or any such thing, but that she should be holy and without blemish." The Greek word for "spot" is *speelos*. Have you ever had a *speelos* on your tie or shirt or dress? The Lord wants no *speeloses*—no wrinkles, no blemishes of any kind.
- First Peter 1:16 says that I ought to be holy, and Hebrews 12:14 adds that if I don't have holiness, I won't see the Lord.
- I know what God really wants because the book *Education* records, "Higher than the highest human thought can reach is God's ideal for His children. Godliness—godlikeness—is the goal to be reached."[1]
- And *Child Guidance* says, "The Lord requires perfection from His redeemed family. He expects from us the perfection which Christ revealed in His humanity."[2] Woe is me!

Beyond all of these seemingly impossible requirements for the likes of me, I further ought to be loving, patient, kind, and all the other fruit of the Spirit. I ought never to sin, for the Bible says, "My little children, these things write I unto you, that ye sin not" (1 John 2:1, KJV). And if I should discover that I have sinned, I ought never to commit that sin again. In addition, I ought to follow the precepts in all nine volumes of the *Testimonies for the Church*, plus *Counsels on Diet and Foods* and all the rest.

Am I all of the above? Further, is anyone I know all of the above? But there has to be a way to meet all of these requirements, for surely, God wouldn't have set up an impossible standard, a goal that we couldn't reach. So, there must be a way to get from point A, where I am, to point B, where I ought to be. There just has to be a way to please God and be accepted by Him, or the whole plan of salvation would be futile. If there is a heaven that God longs to populate with beings from this planet, then there must be a way to meet heaven's entrance requirements. And the good news is that there indeed is a way.

Revelation 7:9 offers such wonderful encouragement: "After these things I looked, and behold, a great multitude which no one could number, of all nations, tribes, peoples, and tongues, standing before the throne and before the Lamb, clothed with white robes, with palm branches in their hands." This snapshot of future glory tells us that whatever the entrance requirements for heaven are, there *is* a way to meet them. Isn't it wonderful that "a great multitude which no one could number" found the way?

The thief on the cross found the way. Have you ever wondered what that man's name was? The way Scripture identifies him tells us something about his character. *Thief* is the KJV designation for him, as well as *malefactor*. Later versions use words like *robber* and *criminal.* John used the softest term for him. He merely refers to "two others" who were crucified with Jesus. Whatever the case, the important fact is that he found the way. Talk about a deathbed conversion!

But he was a Christian for just a few hours before he died. Was he fully sanctified? Did he really reflect the character of Jesus fully? Had he overcome all his bad thieving habits? Had he really proved himself? These observations and questions are totally irrelevant because of what the Savior told him: " 'Assuredly, I say to you, today *you will be with Me in Paradise' "* (Luke 23:43; emphasis added). Apparently, the way he found was the right way. Jesus said, " 'I am the way,' " and the thief found Jesus, so he found the way!

Two biblical texts suggest a rather amazing thought—that some people will make it into the kingdom by the skin of their teeth. The

New Living Translation puts one of these texts like this: "If the work is burned up, the builder will suffer great loss. The builders themselves will be saved, but like someone escaping through a wall of flames" (1 Corinthians 3:15). The other text, Jude 23, speaks of "others save[d] with fear, pulling them out of the fire." Both these texts suggest that it was close. The idea is that the people these texts mention will just barely make it. Maybe they'll be singed, but they'll be saved. However, they will make it, so there has to be a way.

The Desire of Ages says, "Among the heathen are those who worship God ignorantly, those to whom the light is never brought by human instrumentality, *yet they will not perish.*"[3] So, there has to be a way. And there is.

There is a way

Jesus said it. " 'I am the way' " (John 14:6). So simple. So profound. So thrilling! If it is righteousness that we need, we must remember two things. First, our soy-milk-drinking, tofu-eating, TV-rejecting, church-office-holding, literature-distributing, Bible-studies-giving, abstinent righteousness will never cut it with God, because the best righteousness we could ever develop on our own would be only "filthy rags" righteousness. Second, Jeremiah 23:6 speaks of "THE LORD *OUR* RIGHTEOUSNESS" (emphasis added). This means that He is the Way.

What about perfect obedience to the law of God? Heaven could never open its gates to sometimes obedience or occasional obedience or quite often obedience or even mostly obedience. Perfect obedience to God's law is what it takes. The psalmist directs our attention to the way in words prophetic of Jesus: "I delight to do Your will, O my God, and Your law is within my heart." (Psalm 40:8).

Jesus Christ never once disobeyed. He never once broke God's law. He never once broke His Father's heart. He never once sinned. And all of His obedience is a gift to me when I accept Him, so this makes Jesus the Way.

All of us desperately need acceptance by the Father. Paul wrote, "He has made us accepted in the Beloved" (Ephesians 1:6). Thank God, trembling soul, that Jesus says, "Because I am the Way, you can gain acceptance with the Father. Trust Me."

And what of our need for maturity, for finishing, for completeness in the Christian life? Colossians 2:10 trumpets, "You are complete in Him."

The answer is the same for whatever need one might have. Cleansing. Victory. The fruit of the Spirit. Justification. Sanctification. The colorful colloquialism of Hawaiian locals would describe it perfectly, "He's da Way."

So, the "I am the way" of John 14:6 isn't an oversimplification. And it certainly isn't "cheap grace." Rather, it's the most expensive grace imaginable, because we haven't been purchased with money "but with the precious blood of Christ, as of a lamb without blemish and without spot" (1 Peter 1:19).

By the way, this isn't "new theology." It's the gospel!

After having seven studies about Jesus, one young Buddhist woman was asked how she felt about what she had heard. Her answer, "It's too good to be true." But it *is* the truth. He is the Way and the Truth.

Seventh-day Adventists who have emphasized behavior, performance, obedience, law, standards, rules, and requirements need to know this truth.

Seventh-day Adventists who don't have any joy or assurance in their Christian life need to know this truth.

Seventh-day Adventists who are trusting in their level of achievement or sanctification need to know this truth.

Seventh-day Adventists who are guilty, burdened, condemned, and who are worn out from trying need to understand this truth.

And Seventh-day Adventists who just don't see how they can ever measure up need to know the rich, powerful, saving meaning of these four words, "I am the Way."

I'll tell you what they mean to me. I can be accepted while He is making me acceptable. I can be perfect while He is perfecting me. I can be justified while He is sanctifying me. I can be ready while He is getting me ready. I can be complete while He is completing His work in me.

I can be saved while He is saving me. Is this not what Martin Luther meant when he said, "When I look at myself, I don't see how I can be saved. But when I look at Jesus, I don't see how I can be lost"?

On May 21, 1946, Louis Slotin and seven other men were carrying out a dangerous experiment near Los Alamos, New Mexico. They were working with pieces of plutonium, which produces deadly radioactivity when enough of it is brought together. During the experiment, the pieces were accidentally nudged a little too close together, and a great upsurge of radioactivity filled the room. Slotin moved at once. With his bare hands, he pulled the radioactive pieces apart. But in so doing, he exposed himself to an overwhelming dosage of radiation. Several days later he died. The seven other men recovered.

Jesus came down to this dangerous, deadly earth laboratory where we live. On the cross, He threw Himself on the explosive, destructive force of sin, covering it with His own body so we could escape and live.

There has to be a way to be saved; there just has to be—and, praise God, there is! Jesus' life instead of yours. Jesus' righteousness instead of yours. Jesus' perfection instead of yours. Jesus' sinlessness instead of yours. Jesus' death instead of yours. Offer this to the Father by faith, and see where it gets you.

---

1. Ellen G. White, *Education* (Nampa, Idaho: Pacific Press®, 1952), 18.

2. White, *Child Guidance* (Nashville, Tenn.: Southern Publishing Association, 1954), 477.

3. White, *The Desire of Ages* (Nampa, Idaho: Pacific Press®, 1940), 638; emphasis added.

CHAPTER 5

An Offering Without Blemish

We'll begin this chapter with a pop quiz. Pop quizzes are much easier than full-blown, heavy-duty exams, so, don't be nervous about this quiz. Besides, no one will grade your answers!

Suppose, after the establishment of the Old Testament sanctuary services, one of God's people became convicted of some sin and went to the sanctuary with an offering to be made right with God.

1. Did God instruct the individual to *be* the offering or to *bring* the offering?
2. Did God require that the *offerer* or the *offering* be "without blemish"?
3. Whose life was taken to pay the price of God's broken law, the sinner's or the lamb's?
4. Was it the blood of the sinner or the blood of the lamb that made atonement?
5. Was the sinner justified, cleansed, reconciled with God on the basis of being the right kind of offerer or of bringing the right kind of offering?

Now, please exchange papers. The answers will follow.

The phrase "without blemish" appears in the Bible for the very first time in Exodus 12:5. There, God Himself is giving instructions regarding the Passover offering. He said, " 'Your lamb shall be without blemish.' "

The worshipers' deliverance from death depended on their offering. It had to be "without blemish" because it represented Jesus Christ, " 'the Lamb of God who takes away the sin of the world!' " (John 1:29). They couldn't save themselves. Their only hope of deliverance from Egyptian bondage was sprinkling the blood of an offering. An offering that God specified. An offering "without blemish."

The Bible next uses the term "without blemish" in the context of the sanctuary; specifically, regarding the setting aside of the priests for their work. They were being consecrated, dedicated, and sanctified for their positions of ministry and service. And the prerequisite for all of this? According to Exodus 29:1, an offering "without blemish." (Is it not significant that Peter speaks of believers today as "a chosen generation, a *royal priesthood,* a holy nation" [1 Peter 2:9, emphasis added]? Our consecration, our dedication, our sanctification for our life and ministry comes about in exactly the same way as did theirs—by an offering "without blemish.")

The Old Testament contains other instructions about how sinners could be made right with God through making the right kind of offering in the sanctuary. Forty-six more times those instructions say the offering had to be "without blemish." This was God's idea, God's doing, God's way of "reconciling the world to Himself" (2 Corinthians 5:19).

This expression appears for the very last time in the Bible in 1 Peter 1:18, 19: "Knowing that you were not redeemed with corruptible things, like silver or gold, . . . but with the precious blood of Christ, as of a lamb *without blemish* and without spot" (emphasis added). All the way from Moses to Peter—in fact, from Cain to "the multitude which no one could number"—the focus of salvation is not upon the offerer but upon the offering—the One "without blemish."

Seventy-five feet to glory

Let's visit the sanctuary. In your mind's eye, do you see the outer court, the altar of burnt offering, the laver, and the wonderfully designed tabernacle itself with its two apartments?

Do you see the priests in their God-designed apparel ministering at the altar of burnt offering and washing themselves at the laver so that, cleansed, they could minister in the first apartment of the sanctuary, the Holy Place?

Do you see the beauty, the color, the majesty, the awe, the solemnity of it all?

Do you see the priest examining the offering of one of God's people to make sure the offering is without blemish?

Do you see the repentant one, who, having become aware of his sins, places his hands on the head of the lamb and confesses his sins, thus transferring his sins and his guilt to the perfect, totally innocent, without-blemish offering?

Do you see that it was the lamb whose throat was cut, whose life was taken, and whose blood was then taken into the sanctuary to make atonement and reconciliation?

When worshipers presented their offerings in the courtyard of the sanctuary, they stood approximately seventy-five feet from the Shekinah glory of God in the Most Holy Place. Seventy-five feet to glory. Seventy-five feet into the very presence of God. Seventy-five feet from sinner to saint. Seventy-five feet from condemnation to being made right with God.

Sinners couldn't walk past the table of shewbread, the seven-branched lamp stand, and the altar of incense into the Holy Place by themselves. They couldn't grab the veil that separated the Holy Place from the Most Holy, throw it back, rush into the Shekinah glory, and say, "Here I am with my offering, God. Three days ago I sinned, and I thought I'd better come before I did it again." The all-consuming glory of God would have incinerated any sinner who made it that far.

Only with an offering could sinners span the seventy-five feet into the presence of God. Only with an offering that God thought up. A substitute. A death. The blood of a "without blemish" offering. Not their own sorry selves as an offering, because God had said, " ' "You shall offer of your own free will a male *without blemish. . . . Whatever has a defect,* you shall not offer, for it shall not be acceptable on your behalf. . . . It must be *perfect* to be accepted; *there shall be no defect in it* ' ' "(Leviticus 22:19–21, emphasis added).

Two phrases are absolutely key to understanding the sanctuary and the good news that its services taught. The first is the one we've been mentioning, "without blemish." The New King James Version says several times that Israelite worshippers were to be sure their offerings were "without blemish." The New International Version says some fifty-six times "without defect."

The second key phrase is "make atonement." Scripture uses this phrase nearly seventy times. The bridge that can span the seventy-five feet into the presence of God was called *atonement* or "at-one-ment."

Old Testament believers who understood these two phrases and who brought the God-appointed offering could leave the sanctuary singing, "Nothing between my soul and the Savior." They were clean, forgiven, right with God. They were at one with God and full of peace and joy and assurance. No wonder the psalmist penned the words, "Your way, O God, is in the sanctuary" (Psalm 77:13).

Saved without the blood?

At the close of a gospel service, an intelligent-looking man came to the minister and said, "I don't see any necessity for the blood of Christ in my salvation. I can be saved without believing in His shed blood."

The minister said, "OK, how do you propose to be saved?"

"By following Christ's example," the man said. "That's enough."

The minister responded, "I suppose it is. And you propose to do just that in your life?"

"That is exactly what I am going to do, and I'm sure that it's enough."

"Very well. I am sure that you want to begin right. The Word of God tells us how to do that. I read here concerning Christ, 'Who did no sin, neither was guile found in His mouth' (1 Peter 2:22, KJV). I suppose that you can say that of yourself too?"

The man became visibly embarrassed. "Well," he said, "I can't say that exactly. I have sometimes sinned."

"In that case," the minister said, "you do not need an example, but a Savior; and the only way of salvation is by His shed blood."

There is no question that we need an example. And there is no question that Jesus Christ is the divine Exemplar. I long to be like Him—to be pure like Him, to hate sin as He hates sin, to please the Father as He always pleased the Father, to love as He loved. May the Holy Spirit create a hunger and thirst in each of us to reflect His life and to walk in His steps.

But we need a Savior even more than we need an example. Three sentences from a Buddhist catechism second the hopelessness and the helplessness of the man in the story above: "No one can be redeemed by another. No god and no saint is able to shield a man from the consequences of his evil doings. Every one of us must become his own redeemer."

If my atonement is dependent on my copying the example of Christ, the sinless One, by myself; if I have to execute my own redemption; if I have to work out my own salvation so that I can present it to God as my offering to merit eternal life, of all men, I would be most miserable. Yes, we need an example. But more than anything else, we need a Savior, a Substitute, an Offering without blemish that will be perfectly acceptable to the Father on our behalf.

Ellen White wrote, "In the heavenly courts there will be no song sung, 'To me that loved myself, and washed myself, redeemed myself, unto me be glory and honor, blessing and praise.' "[1] "We can do nothing, *absolutely nothing*, to commend ourselves to divine favor. We must not trust at all to ourselves nor to our good works; but when as erring, sinful beings we come to Christ, we may find rest in His love. God will accept every one that comes to Him trusting wholly in the merits of a crucified Savior."[2]

The book of Revelation mentions only two songs: the song of Moses and the song of the Lamb. And it pictures all the inhabitants of heaven and all of the redeemed singing the same song: " 'You are worthy . . . for You were slain, and have redeemed us to God by Your blood out of every tribe and tongue and people and nation, and have made us kings

and priests to our God; . . . Worthy is the Lamb who was slain to receive power and riches and wisdom, and strength and honor and glory
and blessing!' " (Revelation 5:9, 10, 12).

Behold your offering to God: "The church history upon the earth
and the church redeemed in heaven all center around the cross of Calvary."[3] In order to be right with God, accepted of God, reconciled,
redeemed, saved, the Old Testament believer had to bring an offering.
The plan of salvation in the New Testament is not one whit different
from the plan of salvation in the Old Testament. God requires an offering of One without blemish. God accepts people on the basis of a
"without blemish" offering. This means that today, my offering must
consist either of myself and my attempts to copy the example of Christ
and to work out my own salvation or of the offering of Jesus Christ
that has been provided by the Father, who knew we could never in all
the world provide the offering ourselves.

A crushing test of faith

More than five hundred years before God instituted the sanctuary
services, He laid upon Abraham an extremely heavy test, the offering of
his son Isaac—you know, the one who was to be the means of fulfilling
the covenant blessings. Out of this almost crushing test of faith came
one of the most beautiful revelations of the gospel and the plan of salvation revealed in Old Testament times. For at the very last moment,
even as Abraham raised his arm to kill his son, a voice came from
heaven: " 'Do not lay your hand on the lad, or do anything to him; for
now I know that you fear God. . . .' Then Abraham lifted his eyes and
looked, and there behind him was a ram caught in a thicket by its
horns. So Abraham went and took the ram, and offered it up for a
burnt offering *instead of his son.* And Abraham called the name of the
place, THE-LORD-WILL-PROVIDE; as it is said to this day, 'In the
Mount of the LORD it shall be provided' " (Genesis 22:11–14, emphasis added).

In His Son, God has provided an "instead of" offering. An "in place
of" offering. An "on our behalf" offering. This means that we are "ac-

cepted in the Beloved." Out of His incomprehensible love, God provided an offering that, if we'll accept it, will mean redemption, reconciliation, and eternal life to us.

So many Christians today haven't caught the beauty of this simple truth that brings such relief, and peace, and joy, and freedom in Christ. They obey, tithe, and live healthfully to propitiate the Deity—to please God, to get His favor, to win His approval. "Lord, here is my vegetarianism, and I hope You like it." "Lord, here is my offering to You: no TV in my home, and when You come, I trust You will remember that I don't have one." "Lord, here is my offering to You: I'm living where there is no electricity, which makes me unworldly, and I hope You see this."

Doing these things may be just fine, but the only offering to God that will bring salvation is the Lamb of God, the one He provided to Abraham who was the father of all who believe. Our gracious heavenly Father has provided the perfect Offering, the One "without blemish"—*His Son!* There's no other offering like the One He has provided.

Does this mean that my works don't count? Does this mean that my spiritual growth and sanctification mean nothing? Isn't my obedience worth anything? Doesn't my striving to work out my salvation make any difference to God?

Absolutely, it does. It does as the fruit of your salvation by faith in Jesus Christ, the Offering of God's own providing. But it is not the root. The things I do in loving obedience to Him, the life I live, the growth I attain because of the work of the Holy Spirit is the fruit of the loving, saving offering that God has provided for my salvation. Someone has written, "I cannot work my soul to save, this work the Lord has done. But I will work like any slave for love of God's dear Son."

Someone may object, "Paul wrote that we're to present our bodies 'a living sacrifice, holy, acceptable to God, which is your reasonable service' (Romans 12:1). Doesn't this say that we're supposed to *be* the offering?"

As the army slogan said, "Be all that you can be," and by the grace of God make yourself a gratitude offering, a thank offering, a praise offering to God for the sacrifice He has provided. But we can bring only one *sin* offering, *reconciliation* offering, *atonement* offering that is holy and without blemish, without defect, without flaw—the Lamb of God.

It is of the utmost importance that we remember the truth of how the people in Old Testament times got right with God. They didn't get right with Him by *being* the offering but by *bringing* it. That's how we must do it today too!

I can present my progress, my level of sanctification, my obedience, or my whatever as an offering to God, expecting Him to accept me on the basis of what I've done or what I am. But then I'd have a huge question about what God thinks of me. On the other hand, I can present as my offering to God the "instead of" offering, the "in place of" offering, the substitutionary offering, the Lamb of God offering. There's no question about what He thinks of that offering. This is why Ellen White wrote that we don't need to worry about what God thinks of us but about what He thinks of Christ.

I don't know if the following story is true, but I like it. On a little church in Germany stands a stone lamb. When the church was being built, one of the workers fell from the roof to the ground. His friends climbed down as quickly as they could, expecting to find him dead. But he was virtually unhurt. A lamb had been grazing below, and he'd landed on the lamb, absolutely crushing it. He was so thankful that the lamb saved his life that he chose to carve a stone lamb as a memorial.[4] Christians know what it is to have a Lamb die to save them.

1. Ellen G. White, *Testimonies to Ministers and Gospel Workers* (Nampa, Idaho: Pacific Press®, 1944), 456.

2. White, *Selected Messages,* book 1 (Hagerstown, Md.: Review and Herald®, 1958), 353, 354.

3. White, *Testimonies to Ministers and Gospel Workers,* 433.

4. Paul Lee Tan, *The Encyclopedia of 7,700 Illustrations: Signs of the Times* (Rockville, Md.: Assurance Publishers, 1982), 940.

CHAPTER 6

A Prayer Too Good to Be Prayed

An accused man stands before the judge and jury, his whole future hanging on the next words of the jury's foreman. Then the foreman announces, "Your Honor, we find this man innocent of all charges." The accused is so relieved, so elated, so joyous that he can hardly contain himself. He'll never forget the words of the foreman and the emotions of that moment.

An American has been kidnapped by terrorists. Her captors use every possible means of eliciting sound bites that they can use in their propaganda against America. With unrelenting, nightmarish fury, they heap beatings, sleep deprivation, isolation, brainwashing, and threats of beheading on the hapless hostage. And then it all stops. Is it just the eye of the hurricane passing over with some mocking moments of sunshine and calm before the storm returns again? Then the door to the room in which she's being held bursts open and a masked, AK-47-toting captor says in broken English, "Get your belongings, you swine. We're letting you go. You're a free woman." And the hostage walks away as in a dream.

The boss comes into an employee's office and says seriously, "John, I have two things I want to talk to you about, and it's going to affect you and your family." John swallows and says, "Yes, sir." Then the boss says, "The first thing I want to talk to you about is your promotion to head up your department, and the second thing is a nice, hefty raise." John almost falls out of his chair with relief and excitement.

As the bills mount, the college student is depressed and discouraged. She is considering dropping out because she just can't handle both the financial pressures of all the unforeseen expenses and the heavy study schedule at the same time. To top it off, she is asked to come to the business office right away. It is more like a summons than an invitation. *This is it,* she thinks to herself. *It won't even be my decision.* The business administrator himself is waiting on the other side of the counter to speak to her as she enters the office. "Jennie, I think you're going to like this," he says with a smile and a twinkle in his eye. "Your entire four years of college have just been paid in full." Jennie is ready to blast into orbit without any help from NASA!

The siren on the police car and the flashing blue and red lights have just jolted you over to the edge of the road, almost causing you to run into an embankment. With a pulse pounding like some kind of mutant metronome, you wait the tortured forever (actually, a little more than a minute) until the officer is at your car window asking for your driver's license. He pulls out his pad (is this really happening?), questions you, and finally says, "I'm not going to give you a ticket this time, but . . ." Whew! You never thought you'd hear that.

I am absolutely sure that none of the aforementioned feelings could have equaled, let alone surpassed, those of the disciples when they heard Jesus pray that prayer—the one He prayed just before they left the upper room on that fateful Thursday evening. The one He prayed only a few hours before He was betrayed and arrested in the Garden.

It was a prayer unlike any prayer they'd ever heard Jesus pray. It's the longest recorded prayer that He prayed; it takes an entire chapter—John 17. When He prayed, the disciples were just about to leave the precious moments of fellowship they had shared with Jesus in the upper room and step into one of the darkest, most crushing twenty-four hours of their entire lives. But they entered those hours with clean, washed feet and hearts and with the memory of a prayer that was too good to be prayed.

That Thursday night prayer

This prayer of Jesus contains seven statements about the disciples that I'm sure they could hardly believe when they heard them. *Is He talking to His Father about us?* they must have thought to themselves. "Did you hear what He said to His Father about . . . ?" they had to have asked one another. What joy, what assurance, what relief, what hope His prayer must have brought to their hearts!

In the first of these statements about the disciples, Jesus said to His Father, " 'They have kept Your word' " (John 17:6). People who follow Christ will keep God's Word. Keeping His Word is the fruit that appears in the life of a true believer. Jesus commended the church of Philadelphia because " 'you have little strength, *yet you obeyed my word* and did not deny me' " (Revelation 3:8, NLT; emphasis added).

Jesus said that it is not enough to mouth the words, not enough to talk the talk. " 'He who *does* the will of My Father' " will inherit the kingdom (Matthew 7:21, emphasis added). "Trust and obey, for there's no other way." And in this upper-room prayer, Jesus said to His Father about the disciples, "They have kept Your word." These words fell on the ears of the disciples. They heard them. Who wouldn't like to hear the Savior Himself pray these words about them?

The second wonderful statement that Jesus made to the Father about the Twelve appears in John 17:8: " 'They have believed that You sent Me.' " There is nothing more basic in the plan of salvation than a personal belief in a personal Savior sent by a personal God on our behalf. This is an absolute prerequisite. John 6:40 says, " 'This is the will of Him who sent Me, that every one who sees the Son and believes in Him may have everlasting life.' " And later, John wrote, "Whoever believes that Jesus is the Christ is born of God. . . . These things I have written to you who believe in the name of the Son of God, that you may know that you have eternal life" (1 John 5:1, 13). How can we measure the saving importance of belief? Yet in the prayer too good to be prayed, the disciples heard it from Jesus Himself: "They have believed." And the delicious prayer continued.

Notice what came next from the lips of the Lord Jesus Christ: " 'They are Yours' " (John 17:9). The New Living Translation says, " 'They belong to you.' " What did this mean? It meant that Peter, James, John, Andrew, and all the rest were Jesus' sheep, His chosen ones, His children, His people. That's what Jesus said in His prayer. They heard it with their own ears.

Jesus' amazing words concerning the disciples didn't stop. He told the Father, " 'I am glorified in them' " (verse 10). "Father," He was saying, "these fishermen, this zealot, this tax collector, these rough, uneducated Galileans, slow-of-heart-to-believe Philip, doubting Thomas, and the others—glory has come to My name through them."

Even holy angels bend their efforts toward the goal of glorifying God. This is the point of the great controversy and the plan of salvation. Vindicating the name of God and bringing glory to Him before the entire universe is the supreme privilege of every created being. For any being to reach this goal is an amazing accomplishment of the grace of God. And the Lord Jesus Christ counted the disciples as having reached this goal. Because of their lives and because of their love and because they chose to follow Him and stay with Him and walk in His steps and because of their witness, they brought glory to His name! That's what Jesus said to His Father about the disciples.

The wonderment, the relief, and the joy of the disciples must have reached a crescendo when they heard the next thing the Savior said to the Father, " 'None of them is lost' " (verse 12). What agony Jesus must have felt as He followed those words with " 'except the son of perdition.' " It's as if He were saying, "Father, I wanted so much to save all twelve of the disciples, but Judas wouldn't let Me."

There are only two spiritual conditions one can be found in: saved or lost. I am quite sure that the disciples were like us in that they must have wondered many times if they would ever make it. Many people live with the haunting feeling of uncertainty as to whether or not they are in a saving relationship with Jesus Christ even when they are doing their best for Him. But on that Thursday evening, the disciples heard it: "None of them is lost, Father, but one." Blessed disciples. Poor, tragic Judas.

The assurances kept coming in the words of Jesus: " 'They are not of the world' " (verse 14). *The Living Bible* says, " 'They don't fit in with it.' " Christ was saying, "Father, these followers of Mine are different in the way they are supposed to be different. They're really strangers and pilgrims, Father. Their interests and tastes and even their inclinations are not really with the world. They are peculiar. They are separate, as they are supposed to be." What would it mean to you if you could overhear Jesus telling the Father that you are not of the world?

Finally, Jesus prayed, " 'Father, I want those you gave me to be with me, right where I am' " (verse 24, *The Message*). Think of it. A prayer too good to be prayed! "Father, I want these believers, these followers, with Me . . . with Us." They actually heard the words as though Jesus were saying, "I want Peter, James, John, Andrew, Philip, Bartholomew, Matthew, Thomas, Thaddeus, Simon, and James the son of Alphaeus— I want them all with Me. I want Judas also Father, but he doesn't want Me."

This prayer is almost unbelievable! The disciples must have said to each other, "Was Jesus talking about us?" What hope the prayer of Christ must have brought! What assurance! What joy! Truly, it must have been a prayer that was just too good to be prayed. But we don't understand the seven amazing statements Jesus prayed about the disciples until we remember who and what the disciples really were.

The truth about the disciples

I know that some speak of the disciples as Saint Matthew, Saint John, etc. Probably most of us feel that because of their spiritual advantages, living and traveling with the Master for three years, they attained an experience far beyond what any of us can have. Because we are so far removed from them and didn't know them personally, we may tend to feel that they were perfect.

None of us would purposely choose to be overly critical of the disciples, but they were mere human beings who had the same kind of flesh and blood as you and I do. James wrote that even the great prophet Elijah "was a man with a nature like ours" (James 5:17). The disciples' humanity often showed, like ours does. We lose our temper some-times. So did they. We fail on the same point over and over. So did they. We're often slow to make progress, slow to understand, slow to believe. So were they.

Of Philip, it is said that he was "slow of heart, so weak in faith." *The Desire of Ages* reminds us that the apostle John—you know, the one Jesus loved—was a man with an evil temper, a spirit of revenge and criticism and that he was proud, combative, and ambitious to be sec-ond only to Christ in the kingdom.[1] Peter had a big mouth into which he often placed both feet. He made mistakes routinely, and Jesus often reproved him, sometimes rather strongly. James had a rather extensive résumé of negatives, including being called a "son of thunder" and lusting for a high position on Christ's right or left hand.

In that prayer too good to be prayed, Jesus said to His Father of His followers "they have believed." But many times He reproved them for their unbelief, their lack of faith! When He was crucified, they didn't believe He would rise from the tomb. In fact, when Christ was on the cross, they actually doubted His divinity. After all the miracles they witnessed, after all the evidences exhibited of His power, after three years full of beautiful, solid reasons to believe, they still doubted. Yet Jesus said, "They have believed."

In His prayer, the Savior said of the disciples, "They are not of the world." Yet only about three hours before, they were all angry at each other and hardly speaking because of their quarrel about who was go-ing to be the greatest in the kingdom. Doesn't their jockeying for posi-tion, seeking the highest office, and grasping for the inside track smack of the world? Why then could Jesus say to the Father, "They are not of the world"?

When Jesus prayed, "I am glorified in them," doesn't something inside of us make us want to say, "Really, Lord? Are You talking about Your disciples—those rough, uneducated followers?" They still had contempt for Samaritans. That's called racism. Hating was an art form for some of them. Peter had learned a lot of wonderful things from his Master, but he hadn't unlearned how to swear, and just a few hours after Jesus said the words, "I am glorified in them," he let out a string of foul fisherman's oaths. And were they glorifying Jesus when He was taken captive in the Garden and they all forsook Him and fled?

I'm not aiming to detract from the beauty of Christ's prayer and the seven amazing things He said to the Father about the disciples. Rather, I wish to add to the beauty of that prayer by showing what the disciples were like in "real time" when Jesus said what He said and prayed what He prayed. They were falling, failing, flailing human beings. Were they worthy of the sentiments He expressed to the Father? No! Was the work of grace completed in their lives? Hardly. Had they become perfected? Certainly not! And it is exactly this fact that makes the prayer almost incredible.

Why did Jesus, in His prayer, make it sound like they had arrived spiritually?

Some would answer that Jesus prayed that prayer in view of what the disciples would become *after* striving, *after* working out their own salvation, *after* overcoming, *after* the warfare had ended, *after* they had all been martyred. In theological terms, this is called *eisegesis*. It means reading one's own ideas into a passage of the Bible. Think of the disciples thankfully basking in the glow of things Jesus said about them and expressing their gratefulness to Him for His "good heavens-keeping seal of approval." Then imagine how they would have felt if He had responded, "Oh, did you think I was meaning that those things I prayed about you applied to you right now, the way all of you are? I was speaking about when you will finally attain, when you will overcome for sure, when you will indeed become sanctified and sinless."

Despite their failings

The Lord Jesus didn't pray as He did *because of* the disciples' faults and failings. He prayed that way *in spite of* them. The disciples wanted more than anything in the world to be with Him, and that's where they were. They even sinned in His presence, but they were there. (Don't consider this fact as giving us license to sin.) They were with Him, and they stayed with Him. And when they sinned, *He didn't leave them!*

Jesus could pray what He did and say what He did because the disciples were not on an abandoned course of evil—an open, continual, flagrant practice of sin. Falling into sin differs greatly from being immersed in sin and being controlled by it all the time.

Yes, the disciples didn't have much faith. But they had enough to come to Christ and enough to stay with Him. Evidently, they had enough that He could pray, "They have believed."

Why could Jesus pray the John 17 prayer? Because the disciples sought forgiveness when they fell. Because they believed and hoped and trusted in Him. Because they accepted reproof, profited by it, and changed because of it. Because when they strayed, they kept coming back. Because they kept trying to be like Him. Because the trend of their lives, the overall tendency of their lives was toward heaven. Because their overriding purpose was to love Jesus, to serve Him and be faithful to Him.

Some will say this sets too low a standard for the Father's acceptance of us. Others will rejoice because "in Christ," the Father accepts us where we are. But it would be well to remember this, "Peter and his brethren had been washed in the great fountain opened for sin and uncleanness. *Christ acknowledged them as His.*"[2]

Ellen White wrote, "When it is in the heart to obey God, when efforts are put forth to this end, Jesus accepts this disposition and effort as man's best service, and He makes up for the deficiency with His own divine merit."[3] This is why Jesus could pray the prayer that was too good to be prayed. And what relief this prayer must have brought the disciples! What joy! What assurance! What thankfulness! And what a veritable tsunami of love to their blessed Master who made it all possible!

To underscore the glorious thought in the preceding paragraph, think of this: "Christ looks at the spirit, and when He sees us carrying our burden with faith, His perfect holiness atones for our shortcomings. When we do our best, He becomes our righteousness."[4]

Yes, a prayer too good to be prayed. A fact too good to be true. A forgiveness too good to be bestowed. A righteousness too perfect to be shared. A salvation too marvelous to be granted. But the disciples heard those seven affirmations with their own ears. It was "real time," and it was all true!

What if we could hear Christ pray that prayer and know that He was praying about us?

Good news! " 'I do not pray,' " Jesus said, " 'for these alone, but also for those who will believe in Me through their word' " (John 17:20).

If we are trusting in Jesus as they were; if we live in His presence and stay there, as they did; if it is in our hearts to obey God as it was in theirs; if it is our overriding purpose to love Him, serve Him, obey Him, and be faithful unto death as it was theirs, the prayer that was too good to be prayed was prayed for us!

---

1. Ellen G. White, *The Desire of Ages* (Nampa, Idaho: Pacific Press®, 1940), 295.

2. Ibid., 646; emphasis added.

3. White, *Signs of the Times,* June 16, 1890.

4. White, *Selected Messages,* book 1 (Hagerstown, Md.: Review and Herald®, 1958), 368.

CHAPTER 7

Who Is a Saint?

The words *saint* and *saints* are used nearly one hundred times in the Bible. In all of these texts, in all of these multiplied usages, there is one time, and one time only, when a specific individual is called a saint. Can you guess who it might be? You might not believe it if I told you, so I'll quote the text. Psalm 106 rehearses how Israel rebelled against God and sinned openly. Then, in verses 16 and 17, it says, "When they envied Moses in the camp, and Aaron, *the saint of the Lord,* the earth opened up and swallowed Dathan, and covered the faction of Abiram" (emphasis added).

These verses seem incredible to me. The designation of Aaron as a saint immediately follows the mention of Moses, so why doesn't the Bible say "Moses, the saint of the Lord"? If you had to make a list of people who would qualify for being called "saint," would Aaron have even come to mind let alone being on your top twenty list?

What's going on here? Was Aaron different from our usual conception of him, or could it be that the word "saint" means something different than we thought? To examine these questions is to have our eyes opened to whole new expanses of the amazing grace of our Father in heaven and to find new hope and encouragement regarding how He looks at His children, how He actually sees us "in Christ." And when we get a fresh new insight into the mind and heart and love of God, we'll love Him more deeply, trust Him more implicitly, and obey Him more fervently, because love begets love.

Aaron undoubtedly had many good points. Although his brother Moses definitely overshadowed him, he was a very important personage and a giant of a leader—so much so that Ellen White spoke of him as "one of the most illustrious men that ever lived."[1]

She also made a very significant mention of Aaron in connection with Moses: "They were men of great natural ability, and all their powers had been developed, exalted, and dignified by communion with the Infinite One. Their life had been spent in unselfish labor for God and their fellow men; their countenances gave evidence of great intellectual power, firmness and nobility of purpose, and strong affections, . . . and [they] had shared together the signal blessing of God."[2]

Moses himself was so hesitant to respond to God's call for him to lead Israel out of Egypt, so concerned about his ability to communicate effectively as the Lord's spokesperson, that Exodus 4:14 records, "So the anger of the Lord was kindled against Moses, and He [God] said: 'Is not Aaron the Levite your brother? *I know that he can speak well* ' " (emphasis added). Aaron spoke fluent Egyptian. In fact, we are told that he was eloquent. Evidently, he was a good deal more on the cutting edge of Egyptian society than was Moses. After all, Moses didn't have to speak much Egyptian to his sheep.

We must not forget that Aaron was just as much an agent of the miracle-working power of God as was Moses. Exodus 7:10 declares, "Aaron cast down his rod [apparently the rod of Moses] before Pharaoh and before his servants, and it became a serpent." And verse 19 suggests that it was Aaron who took the rod and stretched out his hand over the waters of Egypt when they became blood.

We should also note that God called Aaron just as He called Moses. God asked Aaron to come up into His presence on Mount Sinai. God Himself conferred the priesthood on the family of Aaron and chose Aaron to be the high priest, the very first person to hold that exalted position. In other words, Aaron was no third-string leader. But there was another side to Aaron, "the saint of the Lord." The dark side. The weak side. And it wasn't pretty. The "saint of the Lord" did some very unsaintly things.

Aaron's dark side

There were three major problems, lapses, falls—knowing sins, if you please—that make us raise our eyebrows at the Bible's designation of Aaron as "saint"—at least, with our common misunderstanding of the word *saint*. First, there was Aaron's part in the golden-calf episode. At that time, Moses was in God's presence. He'd been in a summit meeting with the King of kings and Lord of lords on Mount Sinai for more than a month. And the Israelites—the exceedingly impatient, untrusting, spiritually immature called-out ones—wanted a visible leader, not one up in the clouds. They wanted to see something tangible, some kind of representation—never mind the marvelous glory of God on Mount Sinai. The Israelites couldn't see God, and they couldn't see Moses. So they looked to Aaron.

Exodus 32:1 paints the picture of what followed like this: "Now when the people saw that Moses delayed coming down from the mountain, the people gathered together to Aaron, and said to him, 'Come, make us gods that shall go before us; for as for this Moses, the man who brought us up out of the land of Egypt [I thought it was God who brought them out of the land of Egypt], we do not know what has become of him.' "

The crowd turned ugly and demanding, and this is where the unsaintly Aaron appeared. Now it wasn't God first, and courage, firmness, and decision first, and spiritual leadership first. It was weak, wavering, fearing-for-his-own-skin Aaron first.

This is where the golden calf marvelously, mysteriously appeared. At least, that's what Aaron's embarrassing, lame explanation to Moses implied. " 'I said to them, "Whoever has any gold, let them break it off." So they gave it to me, and I cast it into the fire, and this calf came out' " (Exodus 32:24).

In the slanguage of our day, we'd say, "Yeah, right." Think of all that Aaron had to do before the golden calf "came out." He had to collect the gold, design and make the mold, melt the gold, and more. He crafted that golden calf. He made it all happen. God certainly knew it. Moses knew it. And Aaron knew it too. So this "I cast it into the fire, and this calf came out" was a knowing, tragic falsification.

Not only this, but Scripture says that after the golden calf was made, "when Aaron saw it, he built an altar before it. And Aaron made a proclamation and said, 'Tomorrow is a feast to the LORD' " (Exodus 32:5).[3] Disastrous results followed, as happens with the worship of any gods of our own making. Because of their flagrant worship of their visible god, three thousand people lost their lives and their souls under the judgment of God—and all because of the weak, pliant nature of Aaron, the "saint of the Lord." Hmmmmm, do saints sin or something?

We haven't yet mentioned two other well-known sins of this saint. Aaron and Miriam committed one when they became jealous of Moses and said, " 'Has the LORD indeed spoken only through Moses? Has He not spoken through us also?' " (Numbers 12:2). The other occurred when Moses and Aaron became angry at the Israelites and took the glory to themselves instead of giving it to God—not a light departure from God's will and plan. This kept both of them from seeing the Promised Land (see Numbers 20:9–11).

So, how is it that God spoke of Aaron as "the saint of the Lord" when he did so many unsaintly things? It certainly wasn't *because* of his sins, but rather *in spite of* them. God termed Aaron a saint because when He called him, Aaron responded positively and followed Him. Aaron's overriding purpose was to love God, serve God, and obey God. He did so because when Aaron sinned, he acknowledged it, repented of it, confessed it, *and changed.* He did so because Aaron knew all about sacrifices, substitutes, and the efficacy of the blood of a "without blemish" lamb—and he put his faith in the blood of the Lamb. Aaron knew that there was power in that blood. He knew that when he went into the Most Holy Place, his only hope of obtaining God's forgiveness and acceptance was the blood.

What a saint is not . . .

We need to know what a saint is not. A saint is not a person who has died and has been declared a saint by canonization. A saint is not a finally and fully perfected person whom no one can stand to be around. A saint is not a person who changes his clothes in a telephone booth and comes out in red and blue leotards with big red letters S and C on his chest, for "Super Christian." A saint is not a last-day, spiritual body-builder who bulks up in 70 years to what it took Enoch 360 years to achieve. A saint is not a graduate from the school of Christ; rather, a saint is more like a lifetime, "professional" student who sits in class every day. A saint is not the perfected one, not the sinless one, not the no-fault one. The idea that a saint is a believer who has all his or her spiritual ducks in a row—really has it all together, has it made—is foreign to the Word of God.

When the apostle Paul used the term *saints* of the people he wrote to in Corinth, and in Ephesus, and in Philippi, and in Colossae, he didn't mean that they had attained moral perfection. He addressed them that way because they believed in the Lord Jesus Christ as their personal Savior and because of their continuing faithfulness, albeit with lapses, to their commitment. Paul used the word *saint* thirty-nine of the sixty-one times it appears in the New Testament. When he wrote his letters to the Corinthian saints, I'm sure he was very much aware of the unsaintly practices and attitudes of the people whom he was addressing. He knew that those "saints" were a work in progress.

Saints are believers who believe their heads off, who believe their hearts out, and who keep on believing and living out their belief. Saints are sinners who come to God and keep coming and never stop coming. Saints are fumbling, failing believers who hate their fumblings and failings, repent of them, confess them, ask God for His empowering to keep them from fumbling and failing again, . . . *and find the power.* Saints are sinners under construction. Ellen White wrote, "Christ is sitting for His portrait in every disciple."[4] Saints are people who have to have many retakes. Saints are sinners whom God is saving.

Let it be known that if someone concludes that the author of this book believes that all people are saints no matter how they live or that it doesn't matter whether people sin or that people can be saved *in* their sins or that saints are nothing more than sinners who have been baptized and who go to church or that the author is an advocate of "sin and live" theology, that someone would be very mistaken.

Actually, being saints is not so much a matter of how people see themselves as it is a matter of how God sees them *"in Christ."* What Numbers 23:21 says is almost too much to take in. Balaam spoke under the overruling inspiration of the Spirit of God when he said, " 'He [God] has not observed iniquity in Jacob, nor has He seen wickedness in Israel. The LORD his God is with him, and the shout of a King is among them.' " How many times had those people rebelled, complained, talked about going back to Egypt, wanted an idol to worship, murmured, and manifested rank unbelief? Yet in His mercy, His grace, and His unfailing love, God wasn't through with them yet. He still counted them as chosen ones, His people.

It's because of this grace of God that Ellen White could write beautiful, reassuring statements such as this: "If you will come to Jesus just as you are, weak, helpless, and despairing, our compassionate Saviour will meet you a great way off, and will throw about you His arms of love and His robe of righteousness. He presents us to the Father clothed in the white raiment of His own character. He pleads before God in our behalf, saying: I have taken the sinner's place. Look not upon this wayward child, but look on Me."[5] This statement reveals how Scripture could call Aaron "the saint of the Lord." It could do so because God looked at Aaron through His Son.

The twenty-dollar bill

I once read the homely story of a renowned speaker who started his seminar by asking who wanted the twenty-dollar bill he held in his hand. When hands started going up, he said, "I'm going to give this twenty-dollar bill to one of you, but first let me do this," and he proceeded to crumple the money. Then he asked, "Who still wants it?" and people kept their hands in the air.

"Well," he said, "what if I do this?" and he dropped the money on the floor and started to grind it with his shoe. He picked it up, now not only crumpled but also soiled, and asked, "Who still wants it?" And people continued to raise their hands.

"My friends," the speaker said, "you have all learned a very valuable lesson. No matter what I did to the money, you still wanted it because what happened to it didn't decrease its value. It's still worth twenty dollars. Many times we are dropped, crumpled, and ground into the dirt by the decisions we make and the circumstances that come our way. We feel as though we are worthless. However, no matter what has happened or what will happen, you will never lose your value in God's eyes. Dirty or clean, crumpled or finely pressed, you are still priceless to Him."

"Aaron, the saint of the Lord." Saint Aaron. Sounds strange, doesn't it? I think the Lord knew it would be more helpful to us if the only person the Bible called a saint was Aaron rather than Moses or Daniel or Paul. We identify a lot more easily with Aaron than with the others. We may be quite a bit more like Aaron than like the others.

So, why did God see fit to designate Aaron as "the saint of the Lord"? Because he never sinned, because he was always faithful, because once he was so named he never did unsaintly things again? No. God did so because Aaron had believed, and he kept on believing. Aaron put his faith in the substitute he offered, in the "without blemish" sacrifice and the blood that he ministered in God's presence, which brought him forgiveness, acceptance, reconciliation, and redemption.

No wonder then that it can be not only "Saint Aaron" but also "Saint _____." (Put your name in the blank.) The devil hates God's rich provisions of grace and love, and he screams at God, "They aren't saints any more than I am, and You know it. This isn't right. You aren't fair. This is unjust of You, God." And God says, "Oh, really? Let Me tell you something, ex-archangel. If you believed in Me as they do, if you trusted Me as they do, if you loved and followed Jesus and endeavored to obey Him as they do, you would still be a saint as they are."

---

1. Ellen G. White, *Patriarchs and Prophets* (Hagerstown, Md.: Review and Herald®, 1958), 427.

2. Ibid., 425.

3. Ellen White said, "It was Aaron 'the saint of the Lord,'. . . that had made the idol and announced the feast." Ibid., 320.

4. White, *The Desire of Ages* (Nampa, Idaho: Pacific Press®, 1940), 827.

5. White, *Thoughts From the Mount of Blessing* (Nampa, Idaho: Pacific Press®, 1956), 9.

CHAPTER 8

When the Load Becomes Really Heavy

"I saw in my dream Christian walking briskly up a highway fenced on both sides with a high wall. He began to run, though he could not run fast *because of the load* on his back. On top of the hill, he came to a cross. Just as he got to the cross, his burden came loose, dropped from his shoulders, and went tumbling down the hill. It fell into an open grave, and I saw it no more."[1]

This classic allegory pictures the main character, Christian, leaving his friends, his hometown, even his wife and children (they didn't want to go) to start on his way to the kingdom. At this early point in his journey, he had already discovered that he was lost—separated from God and headed for eternal destruction, and this discovery had moved him to repentance and confession and had started him on his way to heaven as a different man, a new man. But he still had a load on his back. A burden. It was heavy. Carrying it was hard. It impeded his progress toward his heavenly home. This heavy load didn't fall off his back until he came to the top of a hill, *until he came to the cross.*

Many can relate to this experience because either they've carried the load previously or they're still carrying it. And it is a burden. It is hard to carry. It does impede our progress toward the kingdom. More than this, it robs us of the delight and the sweetness, the joy and the peace that should mark the Christian who is earnestly striving to follow the

Way. Why? Must the Christian walk include bearing this load of guilt, self-incrimination, uncertainty about our salvation, feelings of unworthiness, wondering if we can ever make it? Has our heavenly Father ordained that we always be burdened with striving for our own salvation so that we won't become boastful, proud, or presumptuous—that we be kept in our place somehow?

Not even!

Through the years, a number of people have talked to me about giving up, about throwing in the towel, about letting it all go. They considered the church, the Bible, the commandments, the requirements, the expectations coupled with their own inabilities to be too heavy. They couldn't take the strain anymore. Some were even considering suicide. The gap between the "ought to be" and the "real me" was too great. It was all a heavy burden.

"Once a scoffer taunted Hannah Whitehall Smith, a popular devotional writer of the mid-1800s, with: 'You Christians seem to have a religion that makes you miserable. You are like a man with a headache. He does not want to get rid of his head, but it hurts him to keep it. You cannot expect outsiders to seek very earnestly for anything so uncomfortable.' This was when Hannah responded by writing her classic *The Christian's Secret of a Happy Life* to give practical direction on how to be a happy, overcoming Christian."[2]

Ellen White wrote the following about a woman who was dwelling on failures, mistakes, and disappointments until she was experiencing grief and discouragement . . . a heavy load:

> While I was in Europe, a sister who had been doing this, and who was in deep distress, wrote to me, asking for some word of encouragement. The night after I read her letter, I dreamed that I was in a garden, and one who seemed to be the owner of the garden was conducting me through its paths. I was gathering the flowers and enjoying their fragrance, when this sister, who had been walking by my side, called my attention to some unsightly briers that were impeding her way.

There she was mourning and grieving. She was not walking the pathway, following the guide, but was walking among the briers and thorns. "Oh," she mourned, "is it not a pity that this beautiful garden is spoiled with thorns?" Then the guide said, "Let the thorns alone, for they will only wound you. Gather the roses, the lilies, and the pinks." . . .

It is not wise to gather together all the unpleasant recollections of a past life,—its iniquities and disappointments,—to talk over them and mourn over them until we are overwhelmed with discouragement. A discouraged soul is filled with darkness, shutting out the light of God from his own soul, and casting a shadow upon the pathway of others.[3]

This woman needed to get the heavy load off her back. She needed to look at the Cross.

Why the load becomes heavy

The Christian who feels that Jesus starts us out toward the kingdom but the rest is up to us will be carrying an unnecessary, self-inflicted burden. *Steps to Christ* encourages us with this thought: "Many have an idea that they must do some part of the work alone. They have trusted in Christ for the forgiveness of sin, but now they seek by their own efforts to live aright. *But every such effort must fail.* . . . He is not only the *author* but the *finisher* of our faith. It is Christ first and last and always. He is to be with us, not only at the beginning and the end of our course, but at every step of the way."[4]

To focus on ourselves, our behavior, our level of sanctification, our ways, the work we must do to wash our robes so that we will appear acceptable, is to drain the joy from our walk with the Lord. The Bible does indeed speak of the triumphant ones who "washed their robes," but a subtle danger threatens us here—that we focus on *our* doing the washing instead of *His* doing the washing. It is not ours to make our own robe and then keep it clean. We need Christ's robe, and we can't make it any cleaner than it already is. His robe is a gift that not only makes the wearer appear absolutely spotless to the loving eye of the Father, but it also—praise His name!—cleanses the wearer inside out and outside in. This gift robe affects not only our standing before God (justification) but also our living before Him (sanctification). And to know this, to believe this, to go to sleep on it and wake up on it, is pure joy.

When we look to ourselves for reasons to feel assurance about our salvation, the load on our back becomes extremely heavy because we are so often unfaithful, fickle, and unbelieving. Our moods swing from uncertainty to discouragement to despair or hopelessness. And well they should, for nothing in ourselves commends us to God unto salvation. Not memorizing the books of Daniel and Revelation, not our work at the Community Services center, not going television-less, not reaching the epitome of health reform as taught in *Counsels on Diet and Foods* and *Counsels on Health*—not anything! Martin Luther gave us the key concerning "sanctification-navel-gazing" when he made the statement I quoted earlier: "When I look at myself, I don't see how I can be saved. When I look at Jesus, I don't see how I can be lost." So be it! So believe it!

Why not add the following statement from *Testimony Treasures* to our assurance arsenal? "There are conscientious souls who trust partly to God, and partly to themselves. . . . Such persons toil to no purpose; their souls are in continual bondage [what a load to carry!], and they find no rest until their burdens are laid at the feet of Jesus."[5]

When we are myopic as Christians and our faults and failings loom large and we give voice to our doubts about our weaknesses and our feelings that we'll probably never make it, we need to remember the following insightful comments: "There are thousands today who need to learn the same truth that was taught to Nicodemus by the uplifted serpent. They depend on their obedience to the law of God to commend them to His favor. When they are bidden to look to Jesus, *and believe that He saves them solely through His grace,* they exclaim, 'How can these things be?' "[6]

We must add this powerful observation from *The Acts of the Apostles,* "There are many who, though striving to obey God's commandments, have little peace or joy. This lack in their experience is the result of a failure to exercise faith. [That hurts!] They walk as it were in a salt land, a parched wilderness. [Does this describe anyone you know?] They claim little, when they might claim much; for there is no limit to the promises of God. Such ones do not correctly represent the sanctification that comes through obedience to the truth. The Lord would have all His sons and daughters happy, peaceful, and obedient."[7]

The answer

How can we find peace and joy and become happy and obedient? In the allegory, when Christian looked at the cross, his burden dropped from his shoulders, went tumbling down a hill, and fell into an open grave, and he saw it no more. John Bunyan wrote, "Now Christian's heart was light. He had found relief from his burden. He said to himself, 'He has given me rest by His sorrows, and life by His death.' He stood gazing at the cross, wondering how the sight of the cross could so relieve one of guilt and shame. He no longer felt guilty of anything. His conscience told him that all his sins were forgiven. He now felt innocent, clean, happy, and free. He knew his sins had all been paid for by the death of the One who had died on the cross. They were gone, buried in the Savior's tomb, and God would remember them against him no more forever. He was so thankful and so full of joy that the tears began to flow."[8]

Ah yes! He was crushed by the heavy burden so I wouldn't have to be. Max Lucado put it so expressively in his book *When God Whispers Your Name:*

> Your eyes see your faults. Your faith sees the Savior.
>
> Your eyes see your guilt. Your faith sees His blood.
>
> Your eyes see your grave. Your faith sees a city whose builder and maker is God.
>
> Your eyes look in the mirror and see a sinner, a failure, a promise-breaker. But by faith you look in the mirror and see a robed prodigal bearing the ring of grace on your finger and the kiss of your Father on your face.[9]

Charles Spurgeon, a powerful preacher of yesteryear, said,

He who is a believer in Jesus finds enough in his Lord to
satisfy him now, and to content him for evermore. The believer
is not the man whose days are weary for want of comfort, [and
assurance] and whose nights are long from absence of heart-
cheering thought, for he finds in religion such a spring of joy,
such a fountain of consolation, that he is content and happy.
Put him in a dungeon and he will find good company; place
him in a barren wilderness, he will eat the bread of heaven;
drive him away from friendship, he will meet the "friend that
sticketh closer than a brother." Blast all his gourds, and he will
find shadow beneath the Rock of Ages; sap the foundation of
his earthly hopes, but his heart will still be fixed, *trusting in the
Lord*. The heart is as insatiable as the grave till Jesus enters it,
and then it is a cup full to overflowing. There is such a fulness
in Christ that he alone is the believer's all. The true saint is so
completely satisfied with the all-sufficiency of Jesus that he
thirsts no more—except it be for deeper draughts of the living
fountain. In that sweet manner, believer, shalt thou thirst; it
shall not be a thirst of pain, but of loving desire; thou wilt find
it a sweet thing to be panting after a fuller enjoyment of Jesus'
love. One in days of yore said, "I have been sinking my bucket
down into the well full often, but now my thirst after Jesus has
become so insatiable, that I long to put the well itself to my
lips, and drink right on." Dost thou feel that all thy desires are
satisfied in Jesus, and that thou hast no want now, but to know
more of him, and to have closer fellowship with him? Then
come continually to the fountain, and take of the water of life
freely. Jesus will never think you take too much, but will ever
welcome you, saying, "Drink, yea, drink abundantly, O beloved."[10]

Bunyan's Christian would agree, don't you think?

Do you agree? Should we not then follow the advice of Ellen White? "We should not make self the center and indulge anxiety and fear as to whether we shall be saved. . . . Put away all doubt; dismiss your fears."[11] Let your heart be instructed and cheered with these further words from her pen:

> In order to fight successfully the battle against sin, you must keep close to Jesus. Do not talk unbelief; you have no excuse for doing this. Christ has made a complete sacrifice for you, that you might stand before God complete in Him. God is not pleased with our lack of faith. Unbelief always separates the soul from Christ.
>
> It is not praiseworthy to talk of our weakness and discouragement. Let each one say, "I am grieved that I yield to temptation, that my prayers are so feeble, my faith so weak. I have no excuse to plead for being dwarfed in my religious life. But I am seeking to obtain completeness of character in Christ. I have sinned, and yet I love Jesus. I have fallen many times, and yet He has reached out His hand to save me. I have told Him all about my mistakes. I have confessed with shame and sorrow that I have dishonored Him. *I have looked to the cross*, and have said, All this He suffered for me. The Holy Spirit has shown my ingratitude, my sin, in putting Christ to open shame. He who knows no sin has forgiven me. He calls me to a higher, nobler life, and I press on to the things that are before."[12]

Isn't this what we should do, pilgrim? Then the unbearably heavy load will fall away!

---

1. James H. Thomas, *Pilgrim's Progress in Today's English* (Chicago: Moody Press, 1979), 39; emphasis added.

2. Daniel Augsburger Jr. in *Here We Stand*, ed. Samuel Koranteng-Pipim (Berrien Springs, Mich.: Adventists Affirm, 2005), 218.

3. Ellen G. White, *Steps to Christ* (Hagerstown, Md.: Review and Herald®, 1956), 116.

4. Ibid., 69; emphasis added.

5. White, *Testimony Treasures* (Nampa, Idaho: Pacific Press®, 1949), 2:94.

6. White, *The Desire of Ages* (Nampa, Idaho: Pacific Press®, 1940), 175; emphasis added.

7. White, *The Acts of the Apostles* (Nampa, Idaho: Pacific Press®, 1911), 563.

8. Thomas, ibid., 39, 40.

9. Max Lucado, *When God Whispers Your Name* (Nashville: W Publishing Group, 1994), 95.

10. Source unknown.

11. White, *Steps to Christ*, 72.

12. White, *In Heavenly Places* (Hagerstown, Md.: Review and Herald®, 1967), 276; emphasis added.

CHAPTER 9

Righteousness by Faith and Righteous Living

Jephthah is not exactly a name that parents put at the top of their list when they're thinking of a name for their son. How many even remember the name? Jephthah was the man who made the vow, " 'If You will indeed deliver the people of Ammon into my hands, then it will be that whatever comes out of the doors of my house to meet me, when I return in peace from the people of Ammon, shall surely be the Lord's, and I will offer it up as a burnt offering' " (Judges 11:30, 31).

The "it" who came out the door when indeed the Lord did give Jephthah victory in the battle, just happened to be his daughter, and she was his only child. He was so shocked when he saw her come out of his house that in his grief, "when he realized who it was, he ripped his clothes, saying, 'Ah, dearest daughter—I'm dirt. I'm despicable. My heart is torn to shreds. I made a vow to God and I can't take it back!' " (verses 34, 35, NLT).

Scholars differ as to what actually happened to Jephthah's daughter—whether Jephthah's vow meant that he would offer her as a human sacrifice or whether she was thereby dedicated to "sacred celibacy" for the remainder of her life. Whichever it might have been, and we trust that it was the latter, Jephthah doesn't get high marks for his foolhardy, harebrained vow.

The narrative about Jephthah ends in Judges 12:7. Amazingly, the Bible next mentions his name in Hebrews 11, the "hall of fame of faith" chapter: "What more shall I say? For the time would fail me to tell of Gideon and Barak and Samson and Jephthah, also of David and Samuel and the prophets" (verse 32). The company in which he's mentioned—"David and Samuel and the prophets"—further boggles the mind.

The people mentioned in Hebrews 11 constitute a roster of those who were faith-filled, faithful, in a saving relationship to Jesus Christ, looking for a "better country" and finding it in and through the promises of God. "All these, having obtained a good testimony through faith, did not receive the promise, God having provided something better for us, that they should not be made perfect apart from us" (Hebrews 11:39, 40). All of the people listed here are models of faith. Jephthah is included with the greats such as Abraham and Moses. Does this mean then that he could actually be a prime example of righteousness by faith, of justification by faith? And if so, how in the world can this be? Jephthah will be saved. He'll be in heaven. Why?

Does the Bible say much about him? It mentions him only in Judges 11 and part of chapter 12. Ellen White mentions him once: "A deliverer was raised up in the person of Jephthah the Gileadite, who made war upon the Ammonites and effectually destroyed their power."[1]

Did he have a great spiritual heritage? Not exactly. He "was the son of a harlot" and later, his half-brothers drove him from his father's house because he was "the son of another woman."

Was he some faith giant? He had faith to ask and believe that God could help him win a war against the Ammonites. But one battle? One incident? One major act of faith?

Was he a model of spiritual attainments and sanctification? The Bible mentions nothing that would indicate that.

Judges 11:29 does say, "Then the Spirit of the Lord came upon Jephthah." I like that! So, with God's help, he fought the Ammonites, and "there was a very great slaughter."

We have to face it. Jephthah was a pretty common individual, although he did judge Israel for six years. Suppose we could rate the people listed in Hebrews 11 regarding the quality and quantity of their faith, with one being those with just enough faith to squeak into the kingdom and ten being a definitely superior, deep, strong, constant faith. From what we know of Jephthah, he might have been somewhere from two to four.

Actually, though, I don't wish to find that he was a faith hero—Abraham-like, Daniel-like, ten feet tall in faith. I prefer him to be "just plain Jephthah" so that "just plain Phil" can find some encouragement.

So, why is Jephthah in Hebrews 11, and why will he be in heaven?

The requirements for being in the kingdom are righteousness, holiness, sinlessness, pleasing the Father, keeping the commandments, and unselfish love and service for both God and man. Will Jephthah be there because he met all these requirements?

Jephthah is in Hebrews 11 and he'll be in the kingdom because of the grace of God, the mercy of God, the incredible love of God, and because of Jesus Christ, the unspeakable gift of God. He'll be there because Jesus Christ took Jephthah's place. He lived a sinless life for Jephthah. He pleased the Father perfectly for Jephthah. He kept the Ten Commandments for Jephthah. He bore Jephthah's sins and paid the penalty for them on the cross, suffering even the second death of eternal separation from God. He was raised from the dead in Jephthah's behalf. He became Jephthah's mediator, intercessor, and advocate before the Father. He'll be there because Christ did all this for him, and Jephthah's faith and trust in God made it possible for God to forgive him, reconcile him, cleanse him, empower him, adopt him, and save him *for Christ's sake.*

I don't know how much faith Jephthah had, but evidently he had enough. That's true of anyone who will be there—of everyone who will be there. We'll be there because we are "accepted in the Beloved" (Ephesians 1:6). We will be there, not because of our spiritual attainments, but because of His atonement. We will be there, not because we are deserving, but because He is deserving. We will be in the kingdom, not because of our merits, but because of His. We'll be there because of His works, not ours. Because of His righteousness, not ours. So, however much faith Jephthah had, and he didn't exactly model faith, please let me have as least at much as he did.

What an illustration of grace and love and mercy is Jephthah!

"One short hour"—or less

What kind of plan did God develop for saving us? "Here is a man born in sin. As Paul says, he is 'filled with all unrighteousness.' His inheritance of evil is the worst imaginable. His environment is at the lowest depths known to the wicked. In some way the love of God shining from the cross of Calvary reaches that man's heart [remember Bunyan's Christian]. He yields, repents, confesses, and by faith claims Christ as his Savior. The instant that is done, he is accepted as a child of God. His sins are all forgiven, his guilt is canceled, he is accounted righteous, and he stands approved, justified, before the divine law. And this amazing, miraculous change may take place in one short hour. *This is righteousness by faith.*"[2]

I disagree with the above statement only where the author says, "This amazing, miraculous change may take place *in one short hour.*" At one point, I was assisting in a three-day seminar for pastors on how to lead people to Jesus Christ using a ten-minute presentation called "The Four Spiritual Facts." Elder H. M. S. Richards Sr. was conducting the morning devotionals. Some of the attendees were concerned that ten minutes was too short a time in which to have someone really accept Christ. I told Elder Richards about this and asked him what he thought. In effect, he said, "Why does it need to take that long?" He was right, because, as we saw earlier, the thief on the cross accepted Christ and found salvation in a twenty-two-word exchange—a matter of seconds.

In the book of Romans alone, the apostle Paul uses the word *righteousness* nearly forty times. The righteousness he speaks of is always God's, not ours. Immerse yourself in the words of Romans 5:15–21:

What a difference between our sin and God's generous gift of forgiveness. For this one man, Adam, brought death to many through his sin. But this other man, Jesus Christ, brought forgiveness to many through God's bountiful gift. And the result of God's gracious gift is very different from the result of that one man's sin. For Adam's sin led to condemnation, but we have the free gift of being accepted by God, even though we are guilty of many sins. The sin of this one man, Adam, caused death to rule over us, but all who receive God's wonderful, gracious gift of righteousness will live in triumph over sin and death through this one man, Jesus Christ.

Yes, Adam's one sin brought condemnation upon everyone, but Christ's one act of righteousness makes all people right in God's sight and gives them life. Because one person disobeyed God, many people became sinners. But because one other person obeyed God, many people will be made right in God's sight.

God's law was given so that all people could see how sinful they were. But as people sinned more and more, God's wonderful kindness became more abundant. So just as sin ruled over all people and brought them to death, now God's wonderful kindness rules instead, giving us right standing with God and resulting in eternal life through Jesus Christ our Lord [NLT].

This is righteousness by faith. And it comes as a gift.

A free gift.

What a gift!

Do you realize what we give to Christ? Our sins. Our love for sin. Our broken promises. Our filthy rags. Our secret, evil thoughts. Our idolatrous affection for things outside His will. Our commandment-breaking. Our sins of omission. Our wretchedness.

And His gifts to us? His life. His death. His merits. His worthiness. His sinlessness. His righteousness. His everything!

What kind of exchange is this? What kind of love prompts this kind of giving?

A new name

In college, my wife and I fell in love. I mean "fell"! I wanted her to have my name. She wanted to have my name. And by our mutual love and choice, it happened. Scripture promises, " ' "In those days Judah will be saved, and Jerusalem will dwell safely. And this is the name by which she [any believer] will be called: THE LORD OUR RIGHTEOUSNESS" ' " (Jeremiah 33:16). Even before we loved Him, He wanted us to have His name. Therefore, by faith, each of us can claim, "THE LORD *MY* RIGHTEOUSNESS."

The Word of God repeats this great, grand truth over and over again. Our Father is hoping that we will understand. Hoping that we will grasp it. " 'This is the heritage of the servants of the LORD, and *their righteousness is from Me,'* says the Lord" (Isaiah 54:17, emphasis added).

What blessedness and hope and relief! " 'He [everyone who chooses] shall say, "Surely *in the LORD* I have righteousness and strength. . . . *In the LORD* all the descendants of Israel shall be justified, and shall glory" ' " (Isaiah 45:24, 25, emphasis added).

First Corinthians 1:30 is good news for all who are looking for the way to get to heaven. "It is because of him that you are in Christ Jesus, *who has become for us* wisdom from God—that is, our righteousness, holiness and redemption" (NIV).

Elsewhere, Paul wrote, "What does the Scripture say? 'Abraham believed God [took Him at His word; had faith in Him], and it [his faith] was accounted to him for righteousness' " (Romans 4:3). Four times in the fourth chapter of Romans, we find the same phrasing: "accounted to him for righteousness." This is called righteousness by faith.

In book 1 of *Selected Messages,* Ellen White quoted Romans 4:3–5 and then wrote, "Righteousness is obedience to the law. The law demands righteousness, and this the sinner owes to the law; *but he is incapable of rendering it. The only way in which he can attain to righteousness is through faith.* By faith he can bring to God the merits of Christ, and the Lord places the obedience of His Son to the sinner's account.

Christ's righteousness [loving God, loving fellow human beings, loving God's law] is accepted *in place of* man's failure, and God receives, pardons, justifies the repentant, believing soul, treats him *as though he were righteous*, and loves him as He loves His Son. This is how faith is accounted righteousness; and the pardoned soul goes on from grace to grace, from light to a greater light."[3]

Here is a further definitive statement from the book *Faith and Works:* "Let the subject be made distinct and plain that it is not possible to effect anything in our standing before God or in the gift of God to us through creature merit. Should faith and works purchase the gift of salvation for anyone, then the Creator is under obligation to the creature. Here is an opportunity for falsehood to be accepted as truth. . . . If man cannot, by any of his good works, merit salvation, then it must be wholly of grace, received by man as a sinner because he receives and believes in Jesus. It is wholly a free gift. *Justification by faith* [or righteousness by faith] *is placed beyond controversy.*"[4]

Does this give a new meaning to the sentence "My grace is sufficient for you"? What grace indeed! What love! What a rich provision for our salvation!

Charles Spurgeon, one of the greatest preachers of the nineteenth century, said that at one point in his life, he worried about whether he could exhaust God's grace. Then he compared himself to a little fish in the Thames River, apprehensive lest, drinking so much water each day, it might drink the river dry—to which Father Thames said, "Drink away, little fish, my stream is sufficient for you."

Next he thought of a little mouse in Joseph's granaries in Egypt, afraid that by eating the wheat daily, it might exhaust the supply and starve to death. He imagined Joseph coming along and, sensing the mouse's fear, saying, "Cheer up, little mouse, my granaries are sufficient for you."

And finally, Spurgeon said, he thought of himself as a man climbing some high mountain and dreading that he might exhaust all the oxygen in the atmosphere—to which fear the Creator Himself said, "Breathe away, O man, and fill your lungs full; My atmosphere is sufficient for you." Spurgeon told his congregation that when he felt the sufficiency of God's grace, for the first time in his life he experienced what Abraham felt when he fell upon his face and laughed!

How grand, how all-sufficient, how delicious, how joy-inspiring to taste the elixir of righteousness by faith. "The enemy of God and man is not willing that this truth [justification by faith/righteousness by faith] should be clearly presented; for he knows that if the people receive it fully, his power will be broken. If he can control minds so that doubt and unbelief and darkness shall compose the experience of those who claim to be the children of God, he can overcome them with temptation."[5]

Where righteous living fits in

So, you ask, what about works, standards, the "battle and the march," the "work out your own salvation with fear and trembling," the "you have not yet resisted to bloodshed, striving against sin," the living up to the light, the "therefore you shall be perfect," the "faith without works is dead." What about the "reflecting the image of Jesus fully" requirement, the righteous-living part of the salvation equation?

I thought you'd never ask!

Righteous living is the result of the righteousness-by-faith experience.

Righteous living is the fruit of faith.

Righteous living is what a believer does when he receives the gift of salvation.

Sanctification follows justification, and if it doesn't, there hasn't been any justification.

Righteousness by faith eventuates in righteous living.

Righteousness by faith is not only a covering but also a converting, dynamic, life-changing force within that moves a believer toward the will and ways and works of Christ.

The believer does not live righteously in order to become righteous. He becomes righteous by faith in the righteousness of Christ ("THE

LORD OUR RIGHTEOUSNESS"), and then the power of God makes the righteous living happen.

Righteous living is the outworking of the Matthew 7:17 principle, " 'Every good tree bears good fruit.' "

The following quotation beautifully summarizes the relation between faith and works: "Grace is unmerited favor, and the believer is justified without any merit of his own, without any claim to offer to God. He is justified through the redemption that is in Christ Jesus, who stands in the courts of heaven as the sinner's substitute and surety. But while he is justified because of the merit of Christ, *he is not free to work unrighteousness*. Faith works by love and purifies the soul. Faith buds and blossoms and bears a harvest of precious fruit. Where faith is, good works appear. . . . Christ is the great depositary of justifying righteousness and sanctifying grace."[6]

As we consider this matter of justification and sanctification, faith and works, righteousness by faith and righteous living, we must remember several things. First, whatever work we do after first exercising faith, "it is God who works in you both to will and to do for His good pleasure" (Philippians 2:13). We believe—He works. We have faith—we then give Him permission to do whatever work He wants to do in us.

I'll pose a question to make the second point. Who of us on the face of this planet can make one thing—anything—holy? The answer is obvious: Not one of us! No one! If, then, Paul speaks of "holiness, without which no one will see the Lord," and we must be holy to enter heaven, and I can't make myself holy, how will I be made holy?

There is only One who can make anything or anyone holy—the omnipotent One, the Creator God, the Re-Creator God. If people try with gritted teeth and with might and main to make themselves holy by their diet, fasting, abstaining, working their heads off, sweating, rigid worship practices, adherence to New Start guidelines, or anything else, these people end up as unholy failures. We can cooperate with God—and we must. But we can't do God's work. His work is to produce holiness in His people. Jesus Christ sanctified Himself so that He could sanctify His people.

Third, God is not only the Author but also the Finisher of our faith. "Being confident of this very thing, that He who has begun a good work in you will complete it until the day of Jesus Christ" (Philippians 1:6).

Do you realize what all of this means? It means that we can be *ready* while He is making us ready. We can be *justified* while He is sanctifying us. We can be *complete* while He is completing us. We can be *accepted* while He is making us acceptable. We can be *perfect* while He is perfecting us. The devil knows that if we believe this, his power will be broken because we will have such rest, peace, joy, confidence, steadfastness, and assurance in Christ that nothing can move us, and he will have to get lost without us.

1. Ellen G. White, *Patriarchs and Prophets* (Nampa, Idaho: Pacific Press®, 1958), 558.

2. Arthur G. Daniells, *Christ Our Righteousness* (Hagerstown, Md.: Review and Herald®, 1926), 15.

3. White, *Selected Messages*, book 1 (Hagerstown, Md.: Review and Herald®, 1958), 367; emphasis added.

4. White, *Faith and Works* (Nashville: Southern Publishing Association, 1979), 19, 20; emphasis added.

5. White, *Gospel Workers* (Hagerstown, Md.: Review and Herald®, 1915), 161.

6. White, *Selected Messages*, book 1, 398; emphasis added.

CHAPTER 10

The Greatest Cover-up in the Universe

It all started in a garden. Adam and Eve themselves were perfect in form, in appearance, in character, and in their oneness. The garden itself, their home, was perfect. The scenery, the birds and animals, the trees for food, the climate, the entire ecosystem, everything was perfect. And their relationship with their Creator God was perfect. So, what was there not to like?

But it was in that perfect place with those perfect people that we all got into it. There began the record of sin, the start of a terrible estrangement from God. And really, it all seems so innocent, perhaps even trivial to us at this point. Six thousand years of sin, alienation, rebellion, disobedience, and total depravity might well make that first sin appear innocent and trivial. However, in the eyes of God, sin is such a dreadfully revolting evil that a sin is a sin is a sin—even if it's just eating a piece of fruit. But then, if the eating meant a lack of love and trust, if it meant disobedience and rebellion, and if it meant putting a talking snake first and God second, then perhaps we can see the enormity of it all as God sees it.

Anyway, suddenly, everything became imperfect. Fear came. Separation came. Blame came. Curses came. Dying came. Nakedness came. Expulsion from the garden came. But just before Adam and Eve left perfection, God did something for them. Genesis 3:21 tells us, "For

Adam and his wife the LORD God made tunics of skin, *and clothed them*" (emphasis added). In Eden, God launched the greatest cover-up in the universe! There we see the reaction of a God who is nothing but love.

Let's not forget the reaction of the human beings in all of this. Genesis 3:7 recounts, "The eyes of both of them were opened, and they knew that they were naked; and they sewed fig leaves together and made themselves coverings." Don't you wonder what a fourteen-foot-tall man was doing in all those fig leaves? Here is humanity's first pathetic attempt to hide from God their desperate, fallen condition. This was the reaction of people who were nothing but sick.

The attitude behind the motto of the Union Pacific railroad, "We Can Handle It," didn't originate in the twentieth century. It started right there in Eden. It could be called "the fig-leaf syndrome"—*sin-drome,* we might say. Adam's new suit might even have sported a classy label: "Made in Eden by Adam. Hand-stitched by Eve." However, our first parents must have known immediately that fig leaves just wouldn't work, because when they heard the sound of God walking in the garden, "Adam and his wife hid themselves from the presence of the LORD God among the trees of the garden" (Genesis 3:8).

Fig leaves have ever been humanity's idea of cover-up. Fig leaves are the first reaction not only of sinners but also of people who don't understand the gospel. This is true even of longtime church members who are stuck on working out their own salvation. Humanity's ideas and humanity's works are never going to cut it with God. He sees right through them. They won't work. We can't cover ourselves up. We can't fix ourselves up. We have to find God's answer for the fix we're in.

His answer? "The LORD God made tunics of skin, *and clothed them.*" This divine cover-up is the only solution for human beings. This is God's idea. This is His work. This is His solution so that sinful human beings, naked, deformed, guilty, lost, can be covered up so that they will appear acceptable and can be justified, sanctified, and glorified.

Scripture doesn't tell us where God got the "tunics of skin" that He used to clothe Adam and Eve. But is it unreasonable to assume that some animals had to die to provide the covering? Whether or not this is true, we must realize that human beings are the only beings in the world who don't naturally furnish their own clothing. All creatures other than human beings grow their own clothing. Not so with people. We are dependent. Ours has to be provided somehow. So, every stitch we wear speaks in one way or another of death.

While we, of ourselves, may be able to provide our physical clothing, our spiritual covering couldn't be a human thing. It had to be a God thing. And spiritually speaking, it is an absolute certainty that it took the death of the only-begotten Son of God for the Father to dress us in the robe of Christ's righteousness.

An oft-repeated biblical concept

Interestingly, one of the most beautiful affirmations of God's providing for our spiritual nakedness comes from the Old Testament. Aptly enough, the whole chapter where it's found has to do with the Messiah, with Jesus. In this setting, Zion, God's people, declares, "I will greatly rejoice in the LORD, my soul shall be joyful in my God; for He has *clothed me* with the garments of salvation, He has *covered me* with the robe of righteousness, as a bridegroom decks himself with ornaments, and as a bride adorns herself with her jewels" (Isaiah 61:10, emphasis added). *The Message* translation says, "He *dressed me up* in a suit of salvation, he *outfitted me* in a robe of righteousness." Praise God! What a heart-boggling cover-up gift from the Father!

Want more?

Zechariah, an additional Old Testament source (the robe of Christ's righteousness is not just a New Testament concept) paints this beautiful picture of the divine cover-up:

> Then he showed me Joshua the high priest standing before the Angel of the LORD [Jesus], and Satan standing at his right hand to oppose him [a graphic picture of the great controversy between Christ and Satan]. And the LORD said to Satan, "The LORD rebuke you, Satan! The LORD who has chosen Jerusalem

rebuke you! Is this [Joshua] not a brand plucked from the fire?" Now Joshua was clothed with filthy garments [his own covering, his own works, his own righteousness], and was standing before the Angel. Then He [Jesus] answered and spoke to those who stood before Him, saying, "Take away the filthy garments [Joshua's filthy-rags righteousness] from him." And to him [Joshua] He said, "See, I have removed your iniquity from you, and I will clothe you with rich robes." And I said, "Let them put a clean turban on his head." So they put a clean turban on his head, and they put the clothes on him. And the Angel of the LORD stood by (Zechariah 3:1–5).

The following excerpts from the book *Prophets and Kings* offers hope and assurance:

Zechariah's vision of Joshua and Angel applies with peculiar force to the experience of God's people in the closing scenes of the great day of atonement. . . .

The tempter stands by to accuse them, as he stood by to resist Joshua. He points to their filthy garments, their defective characters. He presents their weakness and folly, their sins of ingratitude, their unlikeness to Christ, which has dishonored their Redeemer. [Remember, these are God's people during the closing scenes. Rather than being "perfected," it seems that they furnish a great deal for Satan to point at.] He endeavors to affright them with the thought that their case is hopeless, that the stain of their defilement will never be washed away. He hopes so to destroy their faith that they will yield to his temptations, and turn from their allegiance to God. [Here's the reason we are admonished to understand righteousness by faith: so we can stand through the time of trouble.]

Satan has an accurate knowledge of the sins that he has tempted God's people to commit, and he urges his accusations against them, declaring that by their sins they have forfeited divine protection, and claiming that he has the right to destroy them. He pronounces them just as deserving as himself of exclusion from the favor of God. "Are these," he says, "the people who are to take my place in heaven, and the place of the angels who united with me? They profess to obey the law of God; but have they kept its precepts? Have they not been lovers of self more than lovers of God? Have they not placed their own interests above His service? Have they not loved the things of the world? Look at the sins that have marked their lives. Behold their selfishness, their malice, their hatred of one another. Will God banish me and my angels from His presence, and yet reward those who have been guilty of the same sins? Thou canst not do this, O Lord, in justice. Justice demands that sentence be pronounced against them."

And now comes the cover-up—through the merits, the sinlessness, the righteousness of Jesus Christ:

But while the followers of Christ have sinned, *they have not given themselves up to be controlled by the satanic agencies.* They have repented of their sins and have sought the Lord in humility and contrition, and the divine Advocate pleads in their behalf. He who has been most abused by their ingratitude, who knows their sin and also their penitence, declares: "The Lord rebuke thee, O Satan. I gave My life for these souls. They are graven upon the palms of My hands. They may have imperfections of character; they may have failed in their endeavors; but they have repented, and I have forgiven and accepted them."[1]

The pigpen syndrome

My favorite cover-up story is Jesus' parable of the prodigal son who returned to his father (see Luke 15). It illustrates not just the "fig-leaf syndrome" but also the "pigpen syndrome." Really, there's not a lot of difference between the two.

The prodigal came to his senses, Jesus said. " 'And he arose and came to his father. But when he was still a great way off, his father saw him and had compassion, and ran and fell on his neck and kissed him. And the son said to him, "Father, I have sinned against heaven and in your sight, and am no longer worthy to be called your son." But the father said to his servants, [notice how quickly the father brushed aside the son's prepared speech] "Bring out the best robe [the father's rich, royal robe] and put it on him, and put a ring on his hand [the signet of family belonging] and sandals on his feet" ' " (verses 20–22).

I am reminded of one pastor's comment, "You do the coming; He'll do the saving." Or in this case, "You do the coming; He'll do the covering." It seems that whether you look at Adam and Eve or Joshua the high priest or the prodigal son or the parable of the wedding garment (in which only the covering garment supplied by the king could give access to the wedding supper), God, in His love, mercy, and grace, is always going around covering people so they'll be acceptable. The coming is indeed our business. The covering is His business. If we keep coming, He'll keep covering.

At this point, someone might be feeling that I'm placing too much emphasis on the cover-up aspect and not enough on our doing, our behavior, our performance, our part, our obedience. Let me presume to pose a series of questions and to posit the answers.

"Do you believe obedience is important?"

Yes!

"Are we supposed to be overcomers?"

Absolutely. I don't believe we should be "comer-overs."

"Can a Christian keep God's holy law?"

A firm Yes!

"Do you believe in the 'sin and live' theology?"

No!

"Are our works of any significance?"

Yes, as an *evidence* of our salvation.

"Do you believe in 'once saved, always saved'?"

I can't accept this unbiblical teaching.

"Can we choose to live in open sin and practice it as a way of life and expect the righteousness of Christ to cover us?"

Never!

"Are we supposed to live up to the light we have?"

We had better.

"Do our standards, habits, practices—our lifestyle—make any difference in the whole cover-up process?"

Are you kidding?

"Do you think that God's plan is to save us *in* sin or *from* sin?"

From sin!

Now, back to the cover-up. In three places, Revelation 7 connects the redeemed ones and being clothed with—covered with—white robes (see verses 9, 13, 14). In other words, if there is one thing that Revelation 7 makes clear, it is that all the saints have white robes. These robes represent purity, righteousness, perfection, holiness, commandment-keeping, sinlessness, and pleasing the Father perfectly.

Where did these saints get their robes? We find the answer in the counsel to Laodiceans from the True and Faithful Witness, Jesus Christ: " 'I counsel you to *buy from Me* gold refined in the fire, that you may be rich; and *white garments, that you may be clothed,* that the shame of your nakedness may not be revealed [remember Adam and Eve, Joshua the high priest, and the prodigal son]; and anoint your eyes with eye salve, that you may see' " (Revelation 3:18, emphasis added).

We can get the white robe of righteousness only from Jesus. We *buy* it from Him "without money and without price." We get it for the coming. We get it for the asking. We get it on the basis of our desperate need—it is our need that recommends us to the mercy of God. We get it because we throw ourselves on His unfailing love and grace. We don't get it because of our worthiness but because of our unworthiness. Not because of our merit, but because of His. Inspiration says, "He presents us to the Father *clothed in the white raiment of His own character.* He pleads before God in our behalf, saying: I have taken the sinner's place. Look not upon this wayward child, but *look on Me.*"[2]

So, if I understand it aright (forgive my sanctified imagination), the Father looks at me and says, "Oh, you look so pure, so perfect, so righteous, so holy, so sinless, so in harmony with My law. You are so pleasing to me. Your robe fits beautifully. It looks, well, perfect on you." And the Son looks at me and winks because I know, and He knows, and maybe even the Father knows, that my white robe of righteousness is not of my doing but of His. It's a borrowed robe—yet it's mine because it's a gift from my precious Savior. It just seems to me that if He has a robe for Manasseh, and Samson, and Jephthah, and Gideon, and Rahab the harlot, that He just might have one for you and me. What a glorious, magnificent, cover-up—the greatest cover-up in the universe!

The stale baloney sandwich

I love the illustration that Randy Maxwell borrowed from Bob Benson's book *Come Share the Being*.

> Do you remember when they had old-fashioned Sunday school picnics? It was before air-conditioning. They said, "We'll meet at Sycamore Lodge in Shelby Park at 4:30 Saturday. You bring your supper and we'll furnish the tea."
>
> But you came home at the last minute and when you got ready to pack your lunch, all you could find in the refrigerator was one dried up piece of baloney and just enough mustard in the bottom of the jar so that you got it all over your knuckles trying to get to it. And there were just two stale pieces of bread. So you made your baloney sandwich and wrapped it in some brown bag and went to the picnic.
>
> And when it came time to eat you sat at the end of a table and spread out your sandwich. But the folks next to you—the lady was a good cook and she had worked all day and she had fried chicken, and baked beans, and potato salad, and homemade rolls, and sliced tomatoes, and pickles, and olives, and celery, and topped it off with two big homemade chocolate pies.

And they spread it all out beside you and there you were with your baloney sandwich.

But they said to you, "Why don't we put it all together?"

"No, I couldn't do that, I just couldn't even think of it," you murmured embarrassedly.

"Oh, come on, there's plenty of chicken and plenty of pie, and plenty of everything—and we just love baloney sandwiches. Let's just put it all together."

And so you did and there you sat—eating like a king when you came like a pauper.[3]

And so, folk, we come to the salvation supper of the Lamb, and the King Himself has provided everything rich and satisfying and delicious. The penalty for sin has been paid. The demands of the law have been satisfied. There are ample helpings of the righteousness of Christ, His life, His sinlessness, His perfection, His death, His resurrection, His mediation, and His intercession.

We come to the feast, and we put down our stale baloney sandwich of coming to church quite often or usually giving tithes and offerings or having a ten-minute devotional period several times a week or "I have refrained from speaking crossly to my wife for two days in a row" or "I drink soy milk every once in a while," and we spread it out on the salvation table next to all the rich things the King has provided, and it's nothing! But He says, "I really like your sandwich. Why don't we just put it all together?"

So then, you do the coming. Come to the feast with your on-again, off-again healthful living. Come with your stale, oft-repeated, oft-failed promises. Come with your good little worksies. Come with your abstentions. Come with your frail New Year's resolutions. Come with your filthy-rags righteousness. Come with the exceedingly high standards that you apply most stringently to others.

Don't be embarrassed; just come. Forget about your stale baloney—or your "turk-no-more" substitute—sandwich, and just come. God doesn't need your stale stuff, but you desperately need the rich, abundant, delicious provisions He spreads on the salvation table.

"You cannot gain an entrance by penance nor by any works that you can do. No, God Himself has the honor of providing a way, and it is so complete, so perfect, that man cannot, by any works he may do, add to its perfection."[4]

"Forgiveness, reconciliation with God, comes to us, not as a reward for our works, it is not bestowed because of the merit of sinful men, but it is a *gift* unto us, having in the spotless righteousness of Christ its foundation for bestowal."[5]

What a heavenly cover-up!

1. Ellen G. White, *Prophets and Kings* (Nampa, Idaho: Pacific Press®, 1943), 587–589; emphasis added.

2. White, *Thoughts From the Mount of Blessing* (Nampa, Idaho: Pacific Press®, 1943), 9; emphasis added.

3. Bob Benson, *Come Share the Being* (Grand Rapids, Mich.: Zondervan, 1982), 105, 106; quoted in Randy Maxwell, *If My People Pray* (Nampa, Idaho: Pacific Press®, 1995), 52.

4. White, *Selected Messages,* book 1 (Hagerstown, Md.: Review and Herald®, 1958), 184.

5. White, *Thoughts From the Mount of Blessing,* 115, 116; emphasis added.

Chapter 11

A Serious Misunderstanding

In January 2000, city leaders in Charlotte, North Carolina, invited their favorite son, Billy Graham, to a luncheon in his honor. Billy initially hesitated to accept the invitation because he struggles with Parkinson's disease. But the people planning the event said, "We don't expect a major address. Just come and let us honor you." So he agreed to go.

After several wonderful things were said about Dr. Graham, he stepped to the rostrum, looked at the crowd, and said, "I'm reminded today of Albert Einstein, the great physicist who this month was honored by *Time* magazine as the Man of the Century.

"Once, Einstein was traveling from Princeton on a train. The conductor came down the aisle, punching the ticket of each passenger. He came to Einstein, and the great physicist reached in his vest pocket. But he didn't find his ticket, so he reached in his other pocket. It wasn't there, so he looked in his briefcase and still couldn't find it. Then he looked in the seat by him. Not there either.

"The conductor said, 'Doctor Einstein, I know who you are. We all know who you are. I'm sure you bought a ticket. Don't worry about it.'

"Einstein nodded appreciatively, and the conductor contin-ued down the aisle punching tickets. When he was ready to move to the next car, he turned around and saw Einstein down on his hands and knees looking under his seat for his ticket. The conductor rushed back and said, 'Dr. Einstein, Dr. Ein-stein, don't worry. I know who you are. No problem. You don't need a ticket. I'm sure you bought one.'

"Einstein looked at him and said, 'Young man, I too know who I am. What I don't know is where I'm going.' "

Billy Graham continued, "See the suit I'm wearing? It's a brand-new suit. My wife, my children, and my grandchildren are telling me I've gotten a little slovenly in my old age. I used to be a bit more fastidious. So I went out and bought a new suit for this luncheon and one more occasion.

"You know what the occasion is? This is the suit in which I'll be buried. But when you hear I'm dead, I don't want you immediately to remember the suit I'm wearing. I want you to remember this: I not only know who I am, I also know where I'm going."[1]

After fifty-five years of pastoral work, I have concluded that there are far more Seventh-day Adventists who know who they are than who know where they are going. Oh, they know where they want to go. There is no question about their *hope* of going there. But in many doz-ens of visits with believers, I have found that they "believe the truth." They subscribe to the "landmark" teachings of the church. They don't question the Bible, the prophecies, the special end-time prophetic gift to this people, and the singular calling and position of the Seventh-day Adventist Church. They know that we are living in the last days, just before the return of Christ. But when it comes to a personal assurance of present salvation, the knowing stops and the gnawing, chronic, nag-ging uncertainty starts.

Upon being confronted with the question, "Are you saved?" one tortured believer said, "I felt I couldn't stand my unsettled condition much longer. An irrepressible urge to decide whether I was a 'fish' or a 'bird' seized me." *However, many church members are more comfortable when they feel uncomfortable about the present state of their salvation.* There seems to be a mindset that uncertainty is somehow more appropriate, more befitting of humility, and, in a twisted, distorted sense, might even reflect some kind of superior spiritual attainment than actually knowing that one is in a saving relationship to Christ at any particular moment.

The source of this unbiblical belief

What's the source of this comfort with uncertainty about our salvation? I think part of it comes from the unbiblical teaching held by many Christians today that once people are saved, they're always saved no matter what they do or how they live. They are "saved," period. This teaching is commonly known as "eternal security." Adventists have shied away from this belief so strongly that perhaps we have swung too far in the opposite direction, that of "infernal insecurity."

However, I believe that the primary reason for our lack of the assurance of salvation arises from a serious misunderstanding of a few statements that Ellen White made. One is found in the book *Christ's Object Lessons:* "Those who accept the Saviour, however sincere their conversion, should never be taught to say or to feel that they are saved. This is misleading."[2]

The official Ellen G. White Estate Web site addresses this statement under the heading "Statements Taken Out of Context." The Web site says, "A closer look at Ellen G. White's cautions regarding this subject reveals that, in context, *she is not speaking against the certainty of a believer's present standing with God.* She is warning against the presumptuous 'once saved, always saved' teaching of eternal security—those who claim 'I am saved' while continuing to transgress the law of God."[3]

Here is the entire statement from *Christ's Object Lessons:* "Peter's fall was not instantaneous, but gradual. Self-confidence led him to the belief that he was saved, and step after step was taken in the downward path, until he could deny his Master. Never can we safely put confidence in self or feel, this side of heaven, that we are secure against temptation. Those who accept the Saviour, however sincere their conversion, should never be taught to say or to feel that they are saved. This is misleading. Everyone should be taught to cherish hope and faith; but even when we give ourselves to Christ and know that He accepts us, we are not beyond the reach of temptation. God's Word declares, 'Many shall be purified, and made white, and tried.' Dan. 12:10. Only he who endures the trial will receive the crown of life. (James 1:12)."[4]

Twice the above paragraph warns us against the danger of self-confidence. Similarly, it warns us against feeling that we are "secure against temptation" or "beyond the reach of temptation." Does this mean that we ought not to know whether or not we are saved? Let the answer come from the prophet: "Each one of you may *know for yourself* that you have a living Saviour, that He is your helper and your God. *You need not stand where you say, 'I do not know whether I am saved.'* Do you believe in Christ as your personal Saviour? If you do, then rejoice."[5]

The context of the statement in *Christ's Object Lessons* makes it plain that Ellen White's concern was that we might develop a self-confident belief that "I have it made forever," the feeling that we're beyond the reach of temptation. It is as though she was saying, "Don't make the same mistake that many Christians make and believe that once you are saved, you can never be anything else." She wasn't saying that we shouldn't know whether we're in a saving relationship to Jesus Christ.

A further opportunity for a like misunderstanding comes from several passages in book 1 of *Selected Messages*:

> We are never to rest in a satisfied condition, and cease to make advancement, saying "I am saved." When this idea is entertained, the motives for watchfulness, for prayer, for earnest endeavor to press onward to higher attainments, cease to exist. No sanctified tongue will be found uttering these words till Christ shall come, and we enter in through the gates into the

city of God. Then, with the utmost propriety, we may give glory to God and to the Lamb for eternal deliverance. As long as man is full of weakness—for of himself he cannot save his soul—he should never dare to say, "I am saved."[6]

If we are disobedient, our characters are out of harmony with God's moral rule of government, and it is stating a false-hood to say, "I am saved." No one is saved who is a transgressor of the law of God, which is the foundation of His government in heaven and in earth.[7]

If you sit down with the ease-loving ones, with the words on your lips, "I am saved," and disregard the commandments of God, you will be eternally lost.[8]

In each of these brief passages, it is easy to see Ellen White's concerns about the popular belief of "once saved, always saved." That belief poses significant dangers.

- It may produce a self-satisfied condition while we cease to advance in the Christian life.
- It may engender a lack of watchfulness, prayer, and "pressing on to higher ground."
- It may encourage us to forget that we are weak.
- It may tempt us to disobey and to transgress the law of God with impunity.

This popular teaching in the Christian world can easily accommodate sinful practices and thus the violation of God's holy standard of righteousness, His law. It is indeed an insidious, unbiblical doctrine about which believers need to be warned—which is exactly what the servant of God did.

Consequently, the idea of any kind of assurance—much less of security—is a very sensitive, hot-button issue among many Adventist believers. The pastor or the person who speaks of it is immediately suspect in the minds of some. Red flags start waving—or at least caution flags. Attitudinal barriers go up. Pre-conceived opinions kick in. People reach for the off switch.

Why?

First, because the terminology "once saved, always saved" is a default setting for many. Second, because the passages from Ellen White's writings that we've just considered come to mind. Third, because, especially among ultra-conservatives in the church, any kind of assurance conjures up the buzzwords "new theology" or "sin and live" teaching.

However, the assurance of salvation that we can enter into by faith in Christ and His Word and His gospel doesn't mean "assurance forever" or "eternal salvation from now on" or a "forever fixed certainty regardless of lifestyle." But if Christians believe God's Word, if they trust solely in Jesus Christ, they can have the sweet comfort of salvation *now, today, at this moment in time.* This assurance says nothing about tomorrow or two weeks from now or ten years from now or forever, but *now.*

Can we know?

Can we know whether we are indeed Christians? Can we know for sure that we're on the way to the kingdom? Doesn't the gospel offer some smidgen of assurance or certainty? Is the badge of membership in the Seventh-day Adventist Church a gnawing uncertainty about our relationship with Christ and about our salvation? Does our aversion to the unscriptural belief of "once saved always saved" mean that the more uncertain and insecure we are about our present salvation, the stronger, more traditional, and historically Adventist we are? Is the evidence that we've reached the pinnacle of sanctification to be found in the fact that we haven't the foggiest notion whether or not we'd be ready if Christ came today—in fact, that thinking we know would be evidence that we aren't ready? Are we to be known for our "infernal insecurity" concerning our salvation?

Consider what a believer's insecurity is based upon. It is based on self—on looking to self. It is based on my performance, my behavior, my perception of my level of sanctification. It is based on how I think I'm doing, whether or not I think I am where I should be in my Christian walk, on whether I have grown far enough and fast enough, whether I am really worthy of God's acceptance. It is based on whether or not I am all that I should be according to the *Testimonies* and *Counsels on Diet and Foods*. My myopic focus on self totally overshadows the Word of God, the promises of God, His gospel. Little wonder then that Martin Luther said, "When I look at myself, I don't see how I can be saved." And little wonder that there would be no "blessed assurance" but only miserable misgivings.

Don't pin your hope of eternal life on *you!* Pin your hope on *Him!* If you find comfort in gloom, uncertainty, insecurity, discouragement, and that "why-don't-you-give-up-and-quit trying?" feeling, look at yourself, your faults, failings, stumbling, and slowness to be all that you ought to be and there will be comfort enough. If, on the other hand, you want joy, peace, courage, freedom, hope, encouragement, and assurance, look to Jesus. Remember that if you lived another thousand years, all the while growing in grace, overcoming, and putting away sin, *you would be no more worthy of eternal salvation than you are today!*

A personal note: Do you know what I'm counting on for my salvation? I'm counting on a handshake and a hug! *The Desire of Ages* pictures Christ coming into the presence of the Father after His resurrection. The angels and other heavenly beings are anxious to celebrate His triumph, His victory over Satan, and to worship Him.

> But He waves them back. Not yet; He cannot now receive the coronet of glory and the royal robe. He enters into the presence of His Father. He points to His wounded head, the pierced side, the marred feet; He lifts His hands, bearing the print of nails. He points to the tokens of His triumph, He presents to God the wave sheaf, those raised with Him as representatives of the great multitude who shall come forth from the grave at

His second coming. He approaches the Father. . . . Before the foundations of the earth were laid, the Father and the Son had united in a covenant to redeem man if he should be overcome by Satan. *They had clasped their hands in a solemn pledge* [there's the handshake] that Christ should become the surety for the human race. This pledge Christ has fulfilled. . . . The compact had been fully carried out. . . .

The voice of God is heard proclaiming that justice is satisfied. Satan is vanquished. Christ's toiling, struggling ones on earth are *"accepted in the Beloved."* . . . *The Father's arms encircle His Son* [there's the hug], and the word is given, "Let all the angels of God worship Him."[9]

There is no security in my faithfulness, only in His. There is no security in my perfection, only in His. There is no security in my sinlessness, only in His. There is no security in my record, only in His. There is no security in my overcoming, only in His. There is no security in my righteousness, only in His. There is no security in my promises to Him, only in His promises to me. There is no security in how I live for Him and what I do for Him, only in how He lived for me and what He did for me.

If Colossians 2:10 means anything, it means that "you are complete in Him." Verse 9 in the Contemporary English Version says, "God lives fully in Christ," and verse 10 adds, "You are *fully grown* because you belong to Christ," (emphasis added). The Amplified Bible reads, "You are in Him, made full and have come to fullness of life—in Christ you too are filled with the Godhead: Father, Son and Holy Spirit, and *reach full spiritual stature"* (verse 10; emphasis added). The J. B. Phillips translation says, "Your own completeness *is only realized in Him"* (verse 10). And verse 9 in *The New English Bible* reads, "It is in Christ that the complete being of the Godhead dwells embodied, and *in him you have been brought to completion"* (emphasis added).

In Christ by faith; choosing to continue in Christ by faith; thus being complete in Christ by faith—this could make a Christian downright happy . . . in Christ! If we missed claiming this beautiful truth, it would be the most serious misunderstanding of all.

The tragedy is that because of their unfortunate misunderstanding of the inspired statements we have just addressed, too many sincere Seventh-day Adventist Christians are robbed of a peace and joy that is the heritage, the right, the legacy of every believing heart. But there is a vast difference between the false, unjustified, unbiblical, presumptuous assurance of "eternal security" and the sweet, Bible-based, fully justified, Spirit of Prophecy–endorsed assurance that believers can enjoy and revel in through Jesus Christ.

1. Numerous versions of this story appear on the Web; see, John Huffman, *Leadership Journal,* Spring 2003, http://www.christianitytoday.com/le/2003/002/30.69.html.

2. Ellen G. White, *Christ's Object Lessons* (Hagerstown, Md.: Review and Herald®, 1941), 155.

3. Ellen G. White Estate, *Comments Regarding Unusual Statements Found in Ellen G. White's Writings,* http://www.whiteestate.org/issues/faq-unus.html#unusual-section-b1; emphasis added.

4. White, *Christ's Object Lessons,* 155.

5. White, *General Conference Bulletin,* April 10, 1901; emphasis added.

6. White, *Selected Messages,* book 1 (Hagerstown, Md.: Review and Herald®, 1958), 314.

7. Ibid., 315.

8. Ibid., 318.

9. White, *The Desire of Ages* (Nampa, Idaho: Pacific Press®, 1940), 834; emphasis added.

CHAPTER 12

Trusting, Not Trying

The greatest problem of the Christian life is in *trying,* not trusting!

The greatest secret of the Christian life is in *trusting,* not trying!

When Christians are asked, "How is your walk with the Lord?" and they respond, "I'm trying," you can usually know that things aren't great spiritually speaking. It is the trying that brings the sweat to the Christian life. It is the trying that often brings the discouragement. Do you know why? Because we never seem to try hard enough and long enough. It is the focus on trying that again and again makes Christians want to throw up their hands and say, "I've had it." Why? Because it's nothing but hard to try to live a good life, to try to do what you're supposed to do, to try to get your sorry self ready for heaven.

A lovely church I came across once in Southern California had a prominent signboard with an eye-catching statement I will never forget: "When I try, I fail. When I trust, He succeeds." This thought has blessed my heart and influenced my life ever since, and I have shared the blessing with others many times as well.

This saying distills the essence of the gospel. It advocates a focus of faith on Jesus Christ that unlocks the secret of success and joy in the Christian life. If someone should ask us individually how our Christian life is going, we should be able to reply enthusiastically, "Just great—I'm trusting harder every day."

This matter of "trying" in the Christian life generates half a dozen problems. But there aren't a half a dozen answers to those problems. There's just one: *Trusting*—faith in the Lord Jesus Christ, who is 100 percent trustworthy.

We say some children have a hard time growing up. Many Christians also have a hard time growing up spiritually. Isn't it interesting that plants don't seem to have a hard time growing up. In fact, plants don't try to grow. And they certainly don't worry about their growth. Everything that plants need is a gift from God. Sunshine, water, nutrients—all gifts from God. The plants just receive and grow.

Ellen White stated the process so beautifully: "The plants and flowers grow not by their own care or anxiety or effort, but by receiving that which God has furnished to minister to their life. The child cannot, by any anxiety or power of its own, add to its stature. *No more can you, by anxiety or effort of yourself, secure spiritual growth.* The plant, the child, grows by receiving from its surroundings that which ministers to its life,—air, sunshine, and food. What these gifts of nature are to animal and plant, such is Christ to those who *trust* in Him."[1]

So then, Christ is our light, our rain, our food—everything we need for growing up in Him.

The plant's life and the plant's growing are God's responsibility. So it is with the Christian's spiritual growth. It is our choice, our co-operation, but His responsibility. As the Scripture puts it, Jesus is "the author and finisher of our faith" (Hebrews 12:2). We trust Him for spiritual life to begin with, and we trust Him for spiritual growth to continue with. And it is exactly the same with bearing fruit. When I lived in Hawaii, I knew the banana plants weren't *trying* to produce bananas. They just did. A trusting Christian just bears the fruit of the Spirit. As one seminar speaker put it in speaking about fruit bearing, "There I was, walking down the street, just doing what comes spiritually."

Faulty concepts of sanctification

The concept of sanctification that many of us hold has problems. The first problem has to do with the definition of the term. Dictionary definitions say sanctification is "the act of purification from sin," "to make holy, to purify or free from sin." Other phrases we might be familiar with are "continual growth in grace," "the implanting of Christ's nature in humanity," "oneness with God in character," "purity like Christ's purity," "the work of a lifetime." Simply put, it is the *process* of being made holy. That's pretty formidable stuff for us fallen, sinful humans—especially when Scripture adds, "Pursue peace with all men, and holiness, *without which no one will see the Lord*" (Hebrews 12:14, emphasis added).

In relationship to justification, think of sanctification like this:

- Justification is birth. Sanctification is growth.
- Justification is the thief on the cross. Sanctification is John the revelator, who accepted Christ as a young man and lived to be ninety.
- Justification can take place in a thought, in a few moments. Sanctification is the work of a lifetime.

It is important to realize that the sanctification process has to do with holiness of life and character. Here's a question to consider. Can a human being make anything at all holy? Think about it. The answer is overwhelmingly obvious: No! God is the only One who can make anything or anybody holy. If this is the case, should we not consider another way to achieve holiness than by *trying?*

The following statement from *Steps to Christ* underscores this thought: "Many have an idea that they must do some part of the work alone. They have *trusted* in Christ for the forgiveness of sin, but now they seek *by their own efforts* to live aright. But *every such effort must fail!*"[2] Why is this so? Because I am not the sanctifier, Jesus is. Christians do not *try* to work out their own sanctification. They *trust* God to do the work that only He can do.

Christians sometimes feel that justification is beautiful, but sanctification . . . *Look what I have to do. Look what I have to be. Look what I have to overcome. Look at all the things I have to start doing. Look at all the things I have to stop doing. How can I handle all this? I can't!*

But there is good news. Jesus Christ is our sanctification. Paul said so: "Christ Jesus . . . became for us wisdom from God—and righteousness and sanctification and redemption" (1 Corinthians 1:30). The good news is expanded in Acts 26:18. Jesus Himself was outlining Paul's mission, and He commissioned Paul to tell the Gentiles " ' "that they may receive forgiveness of sins and an inheritance among those who are sanctified *by faith in Me*" ' " (emphasis added).

There is even better news, O doubting, misunderstanding Christian. Paul laid out the scenario of faith, of trusting God, in these terms: "May the God of peace *Himself* sanctify you completely; and may your whole spirit, soul, and body be preserved blameless at the coming of our Lord Jesus Christ. He who calls you is faithful, who also will do it" (1 Thessalonians 5:23, 24, emphasis added). Rejoice in *The Message* translation: "May God Himself, the God who makes everything holy and whole, make you holy and whole, put you together—spirit, soul, and body—and keep you fit for the coming of our Master, Jesus Christ. The One who called you is completely dependable. If he said it, he'll do it." Praise God!

We don't become sanctified by *trying*. We become sanctified by *trusting*—trusting the faithfulness and dependability of God. The righteousness that justifies by faith is also the righteousness that sanctifies by faith. The righteousness of Christ that handles our standing before the God of heaven is the very same righteousness that handles our living before God on earth. The righteousness of Christ that starts us on the way to heaven (justification) is the righteousness that keeps us on the way to heaven (sanctification). And this righteousness comes by faith—by *trusting*, not by *trying*.

Faulty feelings

Those for whom living the Christian life means *trying* are constantly looking to self to measure their assurance and whether or not God has accepted them. They live by feelings, not by faith. I remember a woman with whom I was conversing at a potluck in Hawaii. She knew I was a pastor, and she was saying things like "I just don't *feel* that I am a good Christian." "I *feel* that I'm not the Christian I ought to be." "I *feel* I'm not right with God."

I smiled and asked, "Do you remember the Bible verse that says, 'The just shall live by *feeling*'?" From my expression, she knew that I was kidding her. The point is that she was basing her entire Christian experience on feelings, on looking inward to see if she was OK with God—and she never was because in her sight she always fell short even though she was *trying* very hard to live the Christian life.

For all such people, when the spiritual-feelings thermometer is up, they believe they are good Christians, and they feel accepted. And when the thermometer is dropping, they wonder if they are Christians at all. Their experience is like a roller coaster. They lack joy and peace and most of all, assurance.

Steps to Christ, that gem on how to live the Christian life, says, "Your hope is not in yourself; it is in Christ. . . . So you are not to look to yourself, not to let the mind dwell upon self, but look to Christ."[3] "When the mind dwells upon self, it is turned away from Christ, the source of strength and life. . . . Many who are really conscientious, and who desire to live for God, he [Satan] too often leads to dwell upon their own faults and weaknesses, and thus by separating them from Christ, he hopes to gain the victory."[4] "We should not make self the center and indulge anxiety and fear as to whether we shall be saved."[5] Two sentences from *Selected Messages* beautifully continue the thought: "We are not to be anxious about what God and Christ think of us, but about what God thinks of Christ our Substitute. Ye are accepted in the Beloved."[6]

The truth is that you don't live the Christian life by looking to self and *trying*, but rather by looking to Christ and *trusting*.

At this point, some might be alarmed, thinking that I am teaching here that Christians have absolutely nothing to do. Others will be thinking of the text, *"Work out* your salvation with fear and trembling" (Philippians 2:12, emphasis added). And still others will be remembering that Ellen White once described the Christian life as a battle and a march, which of course suggests warring, struggling, and intense effort. For all such, I suggest that Christians can and must do three things: *Believe* (of course, even faith to believe is a gift from God), *choose* (we surely do need to understand the true force of the will in all of this), and *abide*.

John 15:4 gives the key in this sequence: " 'Abide in Me, and I in you. As the branch cannot bear fruit of itself, unless it abides in the vine, neither can you, unless you abide in Me.' " In other words, He was saying "remain united to Me," "dwell in Me," "make your home in Me," "live in Me," "stay joined to Me."

This is where the devotional life of the Christian comes in—meditation, Bible reading and study, prayer, communion, worship. This is how we remain united to Him. And this—one of the few things Christ has commanded us to do ourselves, that is abide in Him—we often do very poorly. Our priorities and our busyness make it so. But it is in the abiding that the union comes—the contact, the strength, the power. *The Desire of Ages* gives this powerful insight: "The life of Christ that gives life to the world is in His Word."[7]

After the Savior admonished us to "abide," He made the cutting-edge revelation that " 'without Me you can do *nothing'* " (John 15:5, emphasis added). However, we surely *try* to do things without Him, because we go for days or weeks or longer on a starvation spiritual diet, without eating the Bread of Life or drinking the Water of Life or picking the fruit (His promises) from the Tree of Life—when all the while our life, our fruit-bearing, our strength, our victory depends upon our abiding. The more we abide, the less we'll *try* and the more we'll *trust.*

Battling the cosmic brawler

Do you know what most Christians *try* to do? They *try* to go into the ring with Satan, to take him on and score a knockout.

Years ago, Anthony Jones was a reporter with *The New York Times*. He was on the hot seat because his writing was flat and colorless; his reporting had no feeling or life. Desperate to hold his job, he came up with the idea of asking Jack Dempsey, then world boxing champion, if he could go into the ring with him. He explained his situation and said that he needed a real-life experience to write about.

At first, Dempsey declined, fearing what might happen to the reporter. Finally, however, he granted the request.

Jones got into the ring with the champ, sparred around a bit, even landing a soft punch—when all of a sudden everything went black. Smelling salts awakened him from his firsthand life experience. Supposedly, Jones reported the incident with such verve and stellar expressions that he kept his job.

So here is Satan, fallen angel indeed, but cunning and powerful— "the prince of the power of the air." Not one of us, in our fallen nature, can last a round with this cosmic brawler. Talk about a mismatch! But we have this concept that Jesus is the trainer: He preps us, sends us into the ring with Satan, and cheers us on. However, when we try that, everything soon goes black for us, and we wake up with the smelling salts of 1 John 1:9, realizing that there was a knockout, and it wasn't Satan who was down for the count.

The incredible reality is that if we ask Jesus, He goes into the ring *for us.* He wins the fight hands down, and we get the benefits and the credit for the victory. His victory is our victory! Our challenge is not to *win* the victory but to *believe and receive* the victory.

So it is that Ellen White wrote, "We cannot, of ourselves, conquer the evil desires and habits that strive for the mastery. We cannot overcome the mighty foe who holds us in his thrall. *God alone* can give us the victory. He desires us to have the mastery over ourselves, our own will and ways. But He cannot work in us without our consent and co-operation. . . . [This is where we must fight and war and strive—to choose His victory.]

"You are not able, of yourself . . . to bring your purposes and desires and inclinations into submission to the will of God; but if you are 'willing to be made willing,' *God will accomplish the work for you.*"[8]

So, here comes a temptation. I have a choice to make. Am I going to handle it myself? Am I going to step into the ring with the devil? Or am I going to ask Jesus Christ to step into the ring for me? If I handle it, I lose. If I choose Christ to go into the ring with the devil, He wins and I win, because He wins every time, and His win becomes my win.

The question becomes, Do I really want the victory? What a struggle! I don't know if I really want the victory or not. I've kind of grown to like smelling salts. If, however, I choose to let Him fight the devil for me, His words ring in my ears, " 'Be of good cheer, I have overcome the world' " (John 16:33).

We can't overcome anything of ourselves. He has overcome everything. If I *trust Him,* He will give me His overcoming as a gift, and His overcoming will be my overcoming. If I *trust Him,* He will give me His victory as a gift, and His victory will be my victory. All of which reminds me of the saying, "I *can't,* and You never said I could. You *can,* and You always said You would."

"When I *try,* I fail. When I *trust,* He succeeds!"

Years ago, Erwin A. Crawford, M.D., wrote an article for *Ministry* magazine entitled "A Chosen Vessel." He used the following illustration:

> I am a fountain pen. I was created for my master's use, and then he bought me and placed me in a cherished place close to his heart where I rest. On occasion he takes me out and tenderly places me in his beautiful hand, and moves me to record his thoughts for the betterment of mankind. I have but one point in life—to be useful to my master. On occasion I become empty—and useless—but he does not cast me aside; he fills me again and again so that I can continue to be useful to him. I can of myself do nothing. I am an instrument for my master's use. Although it is pleasant resting next to his heart, I feel most useful

when my master speaks to others through me. I carefully protect my point so that no defect of mine will mar or deface the thoughts that my master expresses. I do not *try* to do anything by myself, because it is only in partnership with my master that I can contribute. I have no wisdom—he has it all. I have no power—he supplies it. I cannot fill myself—he does it for me. He moves me, and I do not resist or complain. I am an instrument created for my master's use. I am a fountain pen.

The secret of the Christian life is not "I'll *try* my best." It is "I'll *trust* my best." This is where the victory, the joy, and the peace come. And this is where the assurance comes.

1. Ellen G. White, *Steps to Christ* (Hagerstown, Md.: Review and Herald®, 1956), 68.

2. Ibid., 69; emphasis added.

3. Ibid., 70.

4. Ibid., 71.

5. Ibid., 72.

6. White, *Selected Messages,* book 2 (Hagerstown, Md.: Review and Herald®, 1958), 32, 33.

7. White, *The Desire of Ages* (Nampa, Idaho: Pacific Press®, 1940), 390.

8. White, *Thoughts From the Mount of Blessing* (Nampa, Idaho: Pacific Press®, 1956), 142; emphasis added.

CHAPTER 13

The Cleansed Life

Think about this: If you were absolutely clean before God, if you were totally forgiven, accepted of God, pleasing to God, if you were in a state where there was "nothing between [your] soul and the Savior," would you be happy? Would you be at peace with God? And if you were in a position like this and somebody asked you, "If you died tonight, would you be in the kingdom?" what would you be able to say? Wouldn't you be able to give an answer of glad assurance? Wouldn't you have some humble certainty?

Now think about this: What if you could go around in this state, live your life in this assurance, go to sleep in it, and wake up in it. Would you be interested in having this kind of saving relationship with Jesus Christ? Would anyone who is a Christian *not* be interested in this delightsome position? It is possible! It can be a reality! We can live like this every day!

There is no sin so black that it can't be forgiven, no sin so scarlet that it can't be as white as snow, no sin so crimson that it can't be as wool. Let me state it more strongly: No one can commit a sin or even imagine a sin that can't be forgiven—*if* the sinner will repent, confess, and ask for forgiveness.

This thought needs to be still more specific. No matter what example you pick in Bible history, it will only confirm this marvelous truth about God and His forgiveness. Think of

- Adam and Eve and their "little sin" of eating a piece of fruit from the "thou shalt not" tree.
- Levi, who, along with Simeon, avenged Hamor's violation of their sister by killing Hamor, his father, and the men of the city and plundering the city (Genesis 34).
- Manasseh, who committed every conceivable sin of lust, crime, and blasphemy.
- David's sins of adultery and murder and . . .
- Mary Magdalene, "the madam."
- Peter's public, swearing denial of Jesus.

See if you can find a biblical example of people who saw their sin, saw their need, turned to God, confessed, asked for forgiveness, and weren't forgiven. There isn't one. And God will forgive today in exactly the same way. He'll forgive

- the person playing "musical marriages"
- the most hopeless alcoholic
- the young woman who let her boyfriend have sex with her thirteen-year-old daughter to pay a cocaine debt
- the Satanic cult leader
- those who round up children and make them sex slaves

There is no sin so black that God won't forgive it. You can't out-sin the forgiveness of God *if* you truly repent, confess, and ask for forgiveness. This safety net of forgiveness is in no sense a license to sin. It's just a divine reality.

The cleansed life is forgiveness, but it is more than forgiveness. The cleansed life is an extension of forgiveness. All Christians know about forgiveness, but many haven't caught the concept of the cleansed life. It's a way of life, an experience in which we can be clean all the time. *Completely* clean all the time. Man, what a God!

How clean?

Isaiah 1:18, a favorite passage, tells us about clean: " 'Come now, and let us reason together,' says the LORD, 'though your sins are like scarlet, they shall be as white as snow; though they are red like crimson, they shall be as wool.' " The New Living Translation is even more beautiful: " 'Come now, let us argue this out,' says the Lord. 'No matter how deep the stain of your sins, I can remove it. I can make you as clean as freshly fallen snow. Even if you are stained as red as crimson, I can make you as white as wool.' " What a promise! But there's more.

Isaiah wrote, "You have cast all my sins behind Your back" (Isaiah 38:17). And David used a marvelous metaphor to tell what happens to confessed sins. "As far as the east is from the west, so far has He removed our transgressions from us" (Psalm 103:12). We can be this clean!

It is such a relief and matter of rejoicing to read how Micah 7:18, 19 describes God's separation of sin from the repentant sinner: "Who is a God like You, pardoning iniquity and passing over the transgression of the remnant of His heritage? He does not retain His anger forever, because He delights in mercy. He will again have compassion on us, and will subdue our iniquities. You will cast all our sins into the depths of the sea."

God isn't talking about the local duck pond or the neighborhood skating rink that is flooded in the winter. He's speaking about the area in the Hawaiian Islands—the place between Maui and the Big Island that is some five miles deep. He's speaking of the place in the Marianas that is seven miles deep. He wants us to know that when we repent of and confess our sins, He separates them from us and puts them out of sight, which leaves us nothing but clean.

With the Lord and His mercy and grace, there is no end of clean for the sorrowing, sinful human. This is why we are regaled with statements like the following: "He does not see in them the vileness of the sinner. He recognizes in them [amazing grace] *the likeness of His Son*, in whom they believe."[1] "Thus man, pardoned, and clothed with the beautiful garments of Christ's righteousness, *stands faultless before God!*"[2] How clean is this?

However, we have not yet reached the Mount Everest of clean. We must yet revel in 1 John 1:9: "If we confess our sins, He is faithful and just to forgive us our sins and to *cleanse* us from *all* unrighteousness" (emphasis added). If this text ended with "He is faithful and just to forgive us our sins," it would have been wonderfully delicious to the believer. But the verse has a further dimension that is almost beyond our comprehension. The loving Father puts the icing on the promise cake when He adds, "and to *cleanse* us from *all* unrighteousness." So then, how clean does this make the "confessor"? (It is difficult even to write this.) *As clean as Christ!*

So near, so near to God,
I cannot nearer be,
for in the person of His Son,
I am as near as He.

So dear, so dear to God,
I cannot dearer be,
for in the person of His Son,
I am as dear as He.

So clean, so clean in God,
I cannot cleaner be,
for in the person of His Son,
I am as clean as He.

Does God really want to do this for us? Is this His plan for us? Is this His way of relating to His creatures? Is this His actual nature? Does the Father really want members of the sinful human race to be as clean as His Son?

Praise the Lord, the answers are Yes and Amen! God *is* forgiveness. I wish not to say it lightly, but forgiveness is His middle name. Not only is God love (1 John 4:8), but He is also forgiveness. This is what He told Moses when He was showing him His glory, showing him His character, showing him what He is really like (see Exodus 34:7). And in that character delineation, God pronounced grandly "forgiving iniquity, transgression and sin."

Why did God use three words to describe His forgiveness of sin? Because each has a different connotation. *Iniquity* has to do with moral evil. *Transgression* signifies revolt or rebellion. *Sin* means an offence against the Most High God. These three words cover every kind of evil possible. Should we not then be thankful that He used all three words? Whatever the category of sin, He forgives it all. He covers all the bases.

The psalmist wrote, "You, Lord, are good, and ready to forgive" (Psalm 86:5). Striking out the comma after "good" may not make for an accurate translation, but the result accurately portrays the character of God. He is "good and ready to forgive"! In other words, He is good and ready to cleanse us. If we're ready, He's ready.

Do you remember when the leper came to Jesus and said, " 'Lord, if You are willing, You can make me clean' "? Jesus answered him, " 'I am willing; be cleansed' " (Matthew 8:2, 3). The danger threatening the leper was not that Jesus might refuse to cleanse him. The danger was that he wouldn't come to Jesus and wouldn't ask to be clean.

The splendid invitation that Christ directs to us is " 'Come to Me' " (Matthew 11:28). Come with your iniquities, your transgressions, your sins, your faults, your failures, your weaknesses, your guilt. Don't go to a psychiatrist at a time like this. Go to Jesus. *Steps to Christ* adds, "Jesus loves to have us come to Him just as we are," and "It is His glory [His character, the way He is] to encircle us in the arms of His love and to bind up our wounds, to cleanse us from all impurity."[3]

Is it hard to find forgiveness?

The only one who wants to raise an insurmountable barrier to our finding forgiveness is the devil himself. He suggests thoughts like, "How many times would you forgive someone if they alternately slapped you, spit in your face, hit you with their fists, pounded nails through your hands and feet, and drove thorns into your head?"

The beautiful truth is that God isn't like me. " 'For My thoughts are not your thoughts, nor are your ways My ways' " (Isaiah 55:8).

The devil also suggests, "Do you think that God is just going to forgive and keep on forgiving?"

Our answer to this is a resounding Yes.

There is only one situation in which finding forgiveness is difficult. That is if we don't desire it and we don't ask for it. If, however, we desire to be forgiven, confess our sin, purpose to forsake it, and then ask for forgiveness, we will be forgiven and cleansed. *Steps to Christ* assures us of this: "It is peace that you need,—Heaven's forgiveness and peace and love in the soul. Money cannot buy it, intellect cannot procure it, wisdom cannot attain to it; you can never hope, by your own effort to secure it. But God offers it to you as a *gift*, 'without money and without price.' Isaiah 55:1. It is yours if you will reach out your hand and grasp it."[4] Then comes the beautiful follow-up: "If you believe the promise,—believe that you are forgiven and cleansed,—God supplies the fact. . . . It is so if you believe it."[5]

It may be hard for you to forgive yourself, but it isn't hard for God to forgive you. If you doubt this, please ask Mary Magdalene or the prodigal son or the thief on the cross.

Most people don't know God or what He is like or the good news of the gospel, so they don't seek forgiveness. Or, if they do seek it, they most often do so through acts of atonement they themselves perform in order to merit forgiveness. Even among those who know something of God and Jesus, a significant number want a psychologist or a psychiatrist to handle their guilt rather than God. They want this because while they may feel guilty and burdened about something they're permitting or falling upon repeatedly, they know that if they come to Jesus, He wants not only to forgive them but also to *change* them and to *keep them from continuing in that sinful practice.* Some people find this scary because it seems so final—as in "I may never be able to do it again."

We so easily become mixed up about this matter of forgiveness. Many feel that the danger in sinning is that we might "out-sin" God's willingness to forgive us or that He will become fed up with us, tired of our coming, sniveling, asking repeatedly. However, sin's real danger is that it is so virulent, so numbing, that the more we commit it, the less we want to be forgiven and the more disinclined we are to seek God's forgiveness.

A further problem is that we measure God's forgiveness by our own. This can be super discouraging because our middle name is not forgiveness as His is. The apostle Peter represented humanity when he posed the question to Jesus, " 'Lord, how often shall my brother sin against me, and I forgive him? Up to seven times?' " (Matthew 18:21). Undoubtedly, he felt warm all over after he had suggested such a generous number of times for forgiving a person—even more than the norm. Jesus then revealed humanity's problem when he answered Peter, " 'I do not say to you, up to seven times, but up to seventy times seven' " (verse 22). We have our "reasonable" limits, but the Savior has none. Unlimited forgiveness flows out of the beauty of His love and mercy.

Here's another problem that we have with forgiveness: It's harder for us to forgive ourselves than it is for God Himself to forgive us. We are so devastated at our seemingly infinite capacity to sin and miss the mark that we can't conceive of our heavenly Father's infinite, unlimited willingness to forgive us when we desire it and ask for it.

In this connection, we must mention the problem of not "feeling" forgiven even after we have repented, confessed, and asked for forgiveness. It is at this point that the devil weaves a tangled web of lies: "You can't be forgiven now; it's too late." "You've committed this sin too many times." "He could forgive some of your sins, but this one is too black." "Isn't this one more false start that you are making?" "It's obvious that you have out-sinned God's willingness to forgive."

We have a choice. Either we will believe these lies of Satan, who wishes to extinguish our every spark of hope, or we will believe God. *Steps to Christ* tells us what He offers: "It is our privilege to go to Jesus and be cleansed, and to stand before the law without shame or remorse."[6]

The reason there are so many problems with the good news of cleansing is that forgiveness full and free is so precious, so freeing, so encouraging, and it will make us love God so much that we just may wind up staying in His presence forever. Satan hopes that through his lies about forgiveness he can obscure the beauty of God's character, His Word, and the gospel of salvation, and then maybe we'll throw in the towel altogether.

We must remember

Either God is "good and ready to forgive us" or He isn't. We can't earn forgiveness. We can obtain it only as the gift of a God who is full of mercy, grace, and love.

It is so important for us to remember that while we often memorialize each other's sins by etching them in glass that we hang on a wall, engraving them on metal, bronzing them for keepsakes, or recording them on a bracelet that we wear, the Lord Jesus Christ writes our sins in the sand or puts them behind His back or buries them in the deepest ocean. It isn't our sins that He tattoos on His hands to remember, it's our names!

When we have fallen again to the same temptation that has tripped us many times before, the thought enters our minds that perhaps we have committed the unpardonable sin. In those circumstances, we particularly need to remember how Ellen White defined the unpardonable sin. She wrote, "The sin against the Holy Ghost is the sin of *persistent refusal to respond to the invitation to repent.*"[7]

When Moravian missionaries began to bring the gospel to the Eskimos, they couldn't find a word for forgiveness, so they had to make one by compounding several other words. They came up with Issumagijoujungnainermik. "It is a formidable looking assembly of letters, but an expression that has a beautiful connotation for those who understand it. It means 'Not-being-able-to-think-about-it-anymore.' "[8] You can remember either the compounded Eskimo word or Isaiah 43:25, where God says, " 'I will not remember your sins.' "

Think of it. Pardoned. Forgiven. Faultless. Justified. Completely clean. What would this feel like? Ellen White wrote, "In the consciousness of sins forgiven there is inexpressible peace and joy and rest."[9]

Think of the freedom. Think of the release. Think of the load off your shoulders. Think of the assurance you could enjoy.

Living the cleansed life can be a day-by-day, moment-by-moment experience—now . . . tomorrow . . . the rest of this year . . . the rest of your life. Clean. Cleansed. If you so choose.

Are we speaking here of "once saved, always saved"?

Not at all!

Are we looking at sinlessness, sinless perfection, some kind of experience like "holy flesh," never sinning again?

None of this!

What we are speaking of is the first three words of 1 John 1:9, "If you confess . . ." It is vital to understand that confession involves three actions: First, we must agree with the Holy Spirit when He shows us that something we have thought or done is sin. Second, we must acknowledge it—confess it. Third, and most importantly, we must decide, purpose, choose not to continue in that sin any longer. Each of these factors are bound up in the three words "If you confess . . ."

Furthermore, we must understand "spiritual breathing." Exhaling corresponds to confession, and inhaling corresponds to breathing in and claiming the promise of 1 John 1:9: "If we confess our sins, He is faithful and just to forgive us our sins *and to cleanse us from all unrighteousness*" (emphasis added). You just go about exhaling and inhaling, doing "spiritual breathing," as naturally as you breathe physically. In this way, you can live the cleansed life every single moment of every single day.

Does this sound like "sin and live" theology? It's far from it. There is no excuse for sin. We don't have to continue in sin. God can keep us from sin. We can enjoy the victory over any sin. We don't have to be "comer-overs" and yield to temptation. Rather, we can be overcomers, as it is God's plan for us to be.

What we are looking at here is the "old theology" of 1 John 2:1 as expressed in the New Living Translation: "My dear children, I write this to you so that you will not sin. [Amen!] But if you do sin, there is someone to plead for you before the Father. He is Jesus Christ, the one who pleases God completely" (emphasis added). Verse 2 adds, "He is the sacrifice for our sins. He takes away not only our sins but the sins of all the world."

But what if I sin and I'm sorry and confess it and ask for forgiveness, but I really like it and I want to keep on committing, confessing, and continuing? The answer is very simple. The person who prostitutes the grace of God in this way won't have victory, won't have forgiveness, and won't live the cleansed life.

Let me suggest a special assignment. Take a piece of paper and a pen or pencil and ask the Holy Spirit to do what David asked for in Psalm 139:23, 24: "Search me, O God, and know my heart; test my thoughts. Point out anything you find in me that makes you sad, and lead me along the path of everlasting life" (TLB). Ask Him to show you the plague spots in your life—He's the "Divine Pointer-Outer." When He points out something that needs to be different in your life, that needs to be out of your life, write it down.

When He finishes pointing out these dark spots in your character and you finish writing them down, agree with Him that these things are sin. Acknowledge and confess them (exhaling), and purpose that they will no longer be a part of your life. Then, claim 1 John 1:9, "He is faithful and just to forgive us our sins and to cleanse us from all unrighteousness" (inhaling the delicious, clean fragrance of that promise).

You may ask, "Do you mean that if I do this I am cleansed right now?"

No. I don't mean it. Jesus does!

---

1. Ellen G. White, *The Desire of Ages* (Nampa, Idaho: Pacific Press®, 1940), 667; emphasis added.

2. White, *The Ellen G. White 1888 Materials* (Washington D.C.: The Ellen G. White Estate, 1987), 2:898; emphasis added.

3. White, *Steps to Christ* (Hagerstown, Md.: Review and Herald®, 1956), 52.

4. Ibid., 49; emphasis added.

5. Ibid., 51.

6. Ibid., 51.

7. White, quoted in *Seventh-day Adventist Bible Commentary,* vol. 5, ed. Francis D. Nichol (Hagerstown, Md.: Review and Herald®, 1980), 1093.

8. Paul Lee Tan, *Encyclopedia of 7,700 Illustrations: Signs of the Times* (Rockville, Md.: Assurance Publishers, 1982).

9. White, *The Ministry of Healing* (Nampa, Idaho: Pacific Press®, 1942), 267.

CHAPTER 14

Our Hope in the Judgment

The words *judge, judgment, court, verdict, jury, summons, subpoena,* and *ticket* most often seem to have a very negative connotation. As the dreaded red and blue lights were flashing in my rearview mirror, somehow I was thinking about words like these. Let me give the setting so that you can see how truly innocent I was in being set upon in this unseemly manner by an officer of the law who ought to have been spending his time with crimes and criminals.

I was pastoring the Ukiah church in Northern California and was scheduled to conduct a week of prayer at Lodi Academy. (This fact alone would suggest a pristine purity.) Late in the evening, I was making my way, within the speed limit, to my appointment in Lodi. There was more darkness than light as I proceeded to pass a car on the lightly traveled two-lane country road. As I passed the car, I noticed a store on my left and a cross street. Seconds later, all my emotional responses were kicking in as the flashing lights from a police car beckoned—yea, ordered—me to pull over and stop.

The police officer came up to my window, asked for my license, and asked, "Do you know why I stopped you?"

"I haven't the foggiest idea, officer," was my rejoinder.

"You passed a car through an intersection right in the middle of the town."

Town? I thought. *Oh, yes. I did see that store but never gave it a thought.* In any case, I didn't remember anything in the driver's manual about passing a car while driving through an intersection in a . . . *town?*

The officer wrote me a ticket and said I was to see a judge in St. Helena upon my return from my pastoral, spiritual appointment. This untoward incident didn't dampen my enjoyment of sharing and counseling with the students at the academy. But then the week was over, and I returned home under the shadow of my date with destiny and the judge and standing at the bar of justice in St. Helena.

The judge was a very pleasant individual. He began asking me questions, including what my occupation was. (Gulp.)

"I am a pastor, Judge."

He queried further, "In what denomination?"

Was this question germane to anything? Feeling even tenser than I had been, I answered, "The Seventh-day Adventist Church, sir."

Immediately, he said, "Oh, I know a lot of your people up on the hill [the site of Pacific Union College]. Do you know so-and-so and so-and-so and so-and-so?"

I knew them all and began to relax a little in further conversation about the college and his respect for the school and staff members he had met, whether in an official or unofficial capacity, I don't know.

After some minutes of pleasantries, the judge said, "I have never given a ticket to a pastor in my life, and I want you to know that I am not going to start today. But there is one thing I would like to say before you leave. Go, and sin no more!"

I had not hoped for such grace, and as I drove through town and away from St. Helena, it was as a model citizen—one who gave fastidious attention to each and every driving law in the manual.

Before the Judge of all judges

Now the scene quickly changes from a trivial, earthly court to an awesome, heavenly tribunal. Seated on the throne of the universe is the God of gods, the King of kings, the Lord of lords, and the Judge of all judges. " 'I watched till thrones were put in place, and the Ancient of Days was seated; His garment was white as snow, and the hair of His head was like pure wool. His throne was a fiery flame, its wheels a burning fire; a fiery stream issued and came forth from before Him. A thousand thousands ministered to Him; ten thousand times ten thousand stood before Him. The court was seated, and the books were opened' " (Daniel 7:9, 10).

There is absolutely no question about whether there will be a judgment. "He has appointed a day on which He will judge the world in righteousness by the Man whom He has ordained" (Acts 17:31). The apostle Paul wrote, "We must all appear before the judgment seat of Christ, that each one may receive the things done in the body, according to what he has done, whether good or bad" (2 Corinthians 5:10).

There are some things we don't have to do. We don't have to repent, confess, and be converted. We don't have to accept Jesus Christ as our Lord and Savior. We don't have to study the Bible, pray, and join a church. *But we all have to be judged.*

An inspired account in *The Great Controversy* says this: "Every man's work passes in review before God and is registered for faithfulness or unfaithfulness. Opposite each name in the books of heaven is entered with terrible exactness every wrong word, every selfish act, every unfulfilled duty, and every secret sin, with every artful dissembling. Heaven-sent warnings or reproofs neglected, wasted moments, unimproved opportunities, the influence exerted for good or for evil, with its far-reaching results, all are chronicled by the recording angel."[1] And "in the awful presence of God our lives are to come up in review."[2]

While I was living in Takoma Park, Maryland, I had the privilege of visiting the Supreme Court building in Hagerstown, Maryland. I was fortunate enough to arrive just a few minutes before the court convened. Even the building itself tends to move one toward an attitude of awe, respect, and silence. Thinking of the significance of where one is and thinking of the final authority represented there and that resides in the actions of that court was impressive indeed. And then the Supreme

Court justices began to file in. Black robes. Solemn demeanor. It was more than impressive. For Christians, the scene cannot but quickly catapult one into the Daniel 7:9, 10 mode, in which the Ancient of Days is seated and each of us must give an answer before the heavenly tribunal for the lives we have lived.

Such scenes may move us to consider upon what we will base our hope at that most significant, auspicious moment of our lives. Will we base our hope on having finally reached the lofty goal of vegan vegetarianism? Will we base our hope on the level of sanctification we feel we have reached? Will our hope be built upon the fact that we are not nearly as sinful as we used to be? Will our hope be like that of Charles Wesley? When he seemed to be nearing death and a friend asked upon what he rested his hope of eternal life, Wesley replied, "I have used my best endeavors to serve God." Will the strength of our hope consist of the fact that "I am a fifth-generation Seventh-day Adventist"? Will it be based on our flimsy hope that "I am as good as most Christians I know"?

What constitutes the basis of our hope in the judgment is not a trivial matter. It is not something to postpone thinking about. It is something that should claim our considerable, focused attention until we settle it, because it will be either a force that shapes our living and our witness or a dark cloud that hangs over us, leaving us unsettled and tinged with foreboding and trepidation. This is not something we can settle *after* the terminal illness or the fatal accident. This hope needs to be certain, solid, settled, and confirmed *now!*

Our hope in the judgment

Jesus is our hope. Let this be said, and said repeatedly. Writing to his protégé, Timothy, Paul spoke of "the Lord Jesus Christ, our hope" (1 Timothy 1:1). Daniel wrote, " 'I was watching in the night visions, and behold, *One like the Son of Man, coming with the clouds of heaven!* He came to the Ancient of Days, and they brought Him [the One like the Son of Man] near before Him' " (Daniel 7:13, emphasis added). The Son of Man near to the Father for us is our hope.

Our hope is that "the Lamb of God that takes away the sin of the world" is our Judge. " 'The Father judges no one, but has committed all judgment to the Son' " (John 5:22). As Peter preached, " 'He commanded us to preach to the people, and to testify that it is He [Jesus Christ] who was ordained by God to be Judge of the living and the dead' " (Acts 10:42). Inspiration has revealed that "He who occupied the position of judge is *God manifest in the flesh.*"[3]

So, while Scripture portrays the Father as the Chief Justice of heaven's Supreme Court, it also speaks of Christ being our judge. This is no more contradictory than them both being our Creator. Because they are one in character, nature, and purpose, they both are involved in every aspect of the plan of salvation, including the role of judge. They are in it together—and, to me, this only enhances our hope by an exponential factor.

Think of what it means that Christ is our Judge: How many judges are absolutely fair, just, and merciful? How many judges know firsthand what it is like to be condemned? How many judges have received the death sentence? How many judges would step down from the bench (even if it were possible) and take the sentence of the condemned on themselves?

Jesus Christ, our Friend, our Substitute, "the Lover of my soul" is our hope in the judgment. As our Attorney, our Advocate, even our Judge, He will represent us before the Father. "My little children, these things I write to you, so that you may not sin. And if anyone sins, we have an Advocate with the Father [One who pleads for us, represents us, a Helper who speaks in our behalf], Jesus Christ the righteous" (1 John 2:1). "Christ has not entered the holy places made with hands, which are copies of the true, but into heaven itself, now to appear in the presence of God *for us*" (Hebrews 9:24, emphasis added).

What kind of fee are we looking at for the universe's supreme Attorney? Can we afford it? Isaiah assures us, "Is anyone thirsty? Come and drink—even if you have no money! Come . . . it's all free!" (Isaiah 55:1, NLT).

Best of all, His court record shows that He has never lost a case. Once I come and engage this attorney, and I keep desiring for Him to represent me, He promises, " 'I give them eternal life, and they shall never perish; neither shall anyone snatch them out of My hand' " (John 10:28). This is a hope that any believer can take to the bank.

In addition, the Chief Justice of this Supreme Court is this Attorney's Father, and however hopeless the case appears at times, our Advocate finishes His plea with something the Father can't resist. He holds up His scarred hands and points to His head, His feet, and His side, and says, "My blood, Father, My blood," and this settles it. Case closed. Our day in court means our life forever.

Want hope? Our hope rests in the fact that Jesus Christ, our Attorney and our Judge, is also our Brother (see Hebrews 2:11). Can you imagine an earthly court of law permitting a brother of the accused to act as his judge? And this isn't all, because the Father of our Brother is God Himself, so the Chief Justice of the universal Supreme Court *is our Father too*. If that court isn't wonderfully rigged in our favor, I don't know what is.

However, we have not yet reached the top of the Mount Everest of hope in the judgment, for, most of all, our hope centers in the mystery of the gospel, which is that the Lord Jesus Christ meets every demand of the law of God, every requirement of the Word of God. He has perfectly pleased the Father in every instance and has accepted the sentence of death that was rightfully ours. He has paid the price of our penalty (eternal separation from the Father) *and hands all of this to us as a gift!*

"They received it gladly"

A. T. Jones was an able expositor of righteousness by faith at the 1888 General Conference of the Adventist Church. Regarding the ground of our hope in the judgment presented there, he said,

> Some accepted it just as it was given and were glad of the
> news that God had righteousness that would pass the judg-

ment, and would stand accepted in His sight—a righteousness that is a good deal better than anything that people could manufacture by years and years of hard work. People had worn out their souls almost, trying to manufacture a sufficient degree of righteousness to stand through the time of trouble, and meet the Saviour in peace when He comes, but *they had not accomplished it*. These were so glad to find out that God had manufactured a robe of righteousness and offered it as a free gift to every one that would take it, that would answer now, and in the time of the plagues, and in the time of judgment and to all eternity, that they received it gladly just as God gave it, and heartily thanked the Lord.[4]

Amen, and amen!

In one of his recent sermons, Pastor Walter Pearson, speaker of the *Breath of Life* television program, used a powerful illustration that put the quote above into our computer-permeated twenty-first-century understanding. He said that Jesus looks at our list of sins, then He sits at His heavenly computer, and starts going down the list, highlighting, highlighting, highlighting. On and on He goes, clear to the end of our list. And then with the heavenly mouse, He clicks on DELETE! This means our sins are gone, out there in the ether somewhere, "as far as the east is from the west."

But Pastor Pearson's illustration didn't end there. He next pictured Jesus opening up His very own record—blameless, perfect, sinless. And Jesus moves the cursor up, highlights His record, and clicks on COPY. Then He goes back to our record, which is all blank now, and clicks on PASTE. And voilà—be astonished, O heavens, and wonder, O Earth— His record appears as our record! *This is our hope in the judgment!*

If you wish to put your hope in the judgment on

- your deeds, your achievements, your merits,
- your works, your performance, your faithfulness, your obedience,

- your righteousness, your level of sanctification, the perfection that you have developed with blood, sweat, tears, and gritted teeth ("with Jesus' help," of course),
- or the fact that you don't sin in the same way others do . . .

then I wish you lots of luck.

As for this poor, dependent, helpless soul, my hope in the judgment is now and ever will be in Jesus, who is my Attorney, my True Witness, my Judge, my Friend, my Brother, my Savior; my Righteousness, my Sanctification, my Redemption . . . *my Hope.*

In my mind's eye, I can see the devil, his face contorted with hate, in a blind, desperate rage, saying, "Your Honor, I object! This isn't fair. This court is rigged. It is weighted in favor of this miserable defendant."

And then the lovely Jesus lifts His nail-scarred hands to silence him and pronounces before the whole universe, "Objection overruled. This is not only a court of law, but a court of *love.*"

This is the assurance that every single believer can have in Christ Jesus. *He alone* is our hope in the judgment.

1. Ellen G. White, *The Great Controversy* (Nampa, Idaho: Pacific Press®, 1950), 482.

2. Ibid., 490.

3. White, in *Seventh-day Adventist Bible Commentary,* vol. 5, ed. Francis D. Nichol (Hagerstown, Md.: Review and Herald®, 1980), 1134; emphasis added.

4. A. T. Jones, *General Conference Bulletin,* 1893, 243; emphasis added.

CHAPTER 15

A Chosen Child

Scripture repeatedly refers to believers in various ways as children of God. Just what does that mean? The following story tells us in a heart-warming and powerful way:*

Unloved at home, she looked for love in all the wrong places. At fifteen she became pregnant and, abandoned by her family, wandered the streets until she found her way to a home for unwed mothers. On May 19, 1947, she gave birth to a baby boy. I was that unwanted child.

One night my mother slipped away, abandoning me to the care of the state. A few weeks later she married a young man she had picked up in a bar. They came back, retrieved me, and headed west.

My mother's young husband was in the Air Force, and he spent most of the next six years on tours of duty overseas. Lonely and unfulfilled, she spent her nights in the taverns, still looking for love in all the wrong places. She gave birth to five more children, and as the oldest, it fell to me to care for them.

*Excerpted from *The Day I Met God* © 2001 by Jim Covell, Karen Covell, and Victorya Michaels Rogers. Used by permission of Multnomah Publishers, Inc.

My mother was often away for days at a time. Before she left, she would fix a pan of fried cornmeal mush. After that ran out, we would eat ketchup sandwiches or whatever else we could scrounge from the cupboards. All of us slept in one bed on filthy sheets soaked with urine.

As bad as it was when our mother was gone, it was worse when she came home. Often she brought men from the tavern. Some of them verbally or physically abused us. A few of them sexually molested me. I felt abandoned and lonely, but I also felt an overwhelming sense of responsibility for holding my family together. It was an awesome burden for such a young boy to bear.

Then came the catastrophic day when my mother's husband came home from a tour of duty. The apartment was in shambles. We were half-naked and unfed. In a fit of rage, he began to beat her, and she ran from the house. Later the police came. They parceled us out in pairs to my mother's friends from the tavern, and a bitter divorce and custody battle ensured. I never lived with my mother or her husband again.

My first foster parents were both alcoholics, and their home was wracked with violence. He often beat me during his drunken fits, but more often he abused her. One night in a drunken rage, he beat her to death with a hammer.

We were quickly taken from that home and made wards of the state. For five years we were shuffled frequently from house to house. In one house they treated us like animals, punishing us by making us eat out of dog dishes. I was nine years old at the time and still wet the bed. The woman decided that she could break me of the habit by treating me like a puppy. She made me kneel by the bed and then rubbed my face in the urinated sheets. When that didn't work, she showed the sheets to my friends and schoolmates, but her attempts to shame me failed to break me of wetting the bed.

Every night at bedtime I would fervently pray, *God, please don't let me wet the bed again.* Every morning the sheets would be wet. I would pull the covers over the sheets and tell my foster mother that I hadn't wet the bed. At night, I would climb back into bed, the sheets still damp and reeking of rancid urine, for another miserable night of fear and self-loathing.

When I was twelve, the experts declared that I had the sociability of a four-year-old. One of my schoolteachers wrote, "This boy needs to be institutionalized. He will never amount to anything." We had passed through so many homes that I had never figured out who—or whose—I was. More than anything, I wanted a family and a name.

One summer for one magnificent month, all six of us children were together in the same neighborhood. It was the happiest time of my life. Then my two brothers were adopted. On the cruel day that their new parents took them away to Florida, I chased the car down the gravel road, screaming with all my might, "Don't go. Please, dear God, don't let them go." I'll never forget the tearstained faces of my brothers, pressed up against the rear window, as the car sped off into the distance. It was the last time I ever saw them.

I ran to the potato field behind our foster home. Burying my face in the dirt, I wept until I could weep no more. When I got up, I turned my mud-caked face to the sky, shook my fist, and screamed, "God, if You are there, I hate You. I hate You." I had been abandoned too many times.

Though I hated Him, God never stopped loving me.

Across the state lived a childless couple. Arnold was a successful commercial fisherman. His wife, Mary, was desperate for a child. Unable to have children of her own and considered too old to adopt a baby, she went to the state welfare department. The authorities warned her that the only available children were older boys and girls from broken homes. These kids were damaged goods, they said. Adopting any of them was risky business.

But Mary would not be deterred. She wanted a son. They brought her a book filled with the photographs of abandoned children—all wards of the state—and my picture was there. When she saw it among all the others, she said quietly and firmly, "That's the boy I want!"

I'll never forget the day Arnold and Mary Petterson came to our foster home. It was at Christmas time in 1959, and I was twelve years old. I stood shivering in the cold on the front porch, a new pair of shoes pinching my feet. I knew that they had come to check me out and that if they liked me, they just might adopt me. It was the most terrifying moment of my life. I desperately wanted a real family, but I was so sure that they would never choose me.

Then an amazing thing happened. Mary leaped from the car, ran up the sidewalk, pulled me off the porch, encased me in a breathtaking hug, and declared, "Bobby, I love you." No one had ever said "I love you" to me before. It was a moment of delicious ecstasy. More than forty years later, I still get a lump in my throat when I remember that moment.

That afternoon, Arnold and Mary took me bowling. I was sure that if I bowled a couple of strikes, they would like me enough to adopt me. To my dismay, I bowled a string of gutter balls. I was devastated. Who would want a kid who couldn't even knock down a single bowling pin?

Later they took me to a Chinese restaurant. My spirits perked up when I came up with a foolproof plan to redeem the debacle at the bowling alley: I would eat my meal with chopsticks. Surely they would love a kid who could handle chopsticks! To my utter horror, the sticks got tangled up, and I shot a wad of chow mein across the table into Arnold's lap. I was ruined!

But Arnold smiled at me. Deftly flicking the noodles from his lap, he reached under the table and brought out a hand-carved model of his fishing boat. Tears welled up in Mary's eyes. That was their prearranged signal: If Arnold wanted to adopt me, he would give me the boat. Then Arnold asked the question that has never ceased to make me feel humble and grateful: "Bobby, would you like to be our son and become part of our family?" Would I!

A few days later I joined my new family. The first day I went to my new school, some of my classmates taunted me: "You aren't a real kid. Our parents had us the normal way, but you're just an adopted kid." I was heartbroken.

That night, Mary ran her fingers through my hair and soothed my fears. "Bobby," she said, "the rest of those parents had to take what they got from the hospital. But you're extra special. We picked you out of all the children in the world and chose you to belong to us. And chosen children are the most precious ones in the whole world."

Those words were medicine for a wounded soul.

That night I didn't wet the bed. I could scarcely contain the joy and relief I felt when I awakened in a warm and dry bed for the first time in my life. A lifetime of healing was beginning, and the best was yet to come.

During the turbulent sixties, I attended Seattle Pacific University, and one evening while I was a student there, I attended a meeting of Campus Crusade for Christ. The speaker seemed to look directly at me as he spoke of the *aloneness* of a soul apart from God. He talked about hippies—the disenfranchised young people who were joining communes in a desperate search for family. Then he talked about the Father who was searching for lost children to adopt into His eternal family.

I remember his words: "There is someone very special here tonight. Out of all the people in the world, God has chosen you to become a part of His family." Then he talked about the incredible love of this heavenly Father, who had paid the ultimate price by sacrificing His one and only Son to purchase His lost children.

I remembered how Arnold and Mary Petterson had chosen me from among all the photographs in the book of abandoned children. I recalled the incredible price they had paid by investing their lives in me when I had nothing to offer in exchange. I couldn't even bowl or use chopsticks!

Hadn't God done the same—and so much more—for me? He chose me even though I had nothing to offer Him. I would never have to perform in order to earn or keep His love. He loved me even though I had told Him that I hated Him. As special as I was to the Pettersons, I was infinitely more so to God. The Petterson family wouldn't be permanent, and no earthly relationship is ultimately secure, but my heavenly Father would never abandon me, and the family of God would be with me forever. God would never love me any more or any less than He did when He first found me as a lost and broken sinner.

That night I became part of God's family by committing my life to Jesus Christ.

I feel no resentment toward my birth mother. She could have taken the easy way out and had an abortion. Instead, she chose to give birth to me, and when she was incapable of caring for me, she gave me up for adoption. I no longer feel bitterness toward the people or circumstances that made my childhood so traumatic. Instead, I see that those painful experiences gave me a sensitivity that has prepared me for a unique ministry in the lives of countless people around the world.

I no longer feel the despair that I once felt at the loss of my birth family—my five brothers and sisters. Instead, I delight in my countless brothers and sisters in Christ. A few years ago, dear Mary Petterson died, and one day Arnold will join her. Sometimes these losses make me sad, but I've learned that no human family is permanent. The only lasting love is from the Father who chose me to be His child forever.

Three momentous truths

What does this touching story mean to us? It illustrates three mind-boggling truths found in God's Word:

1. God has adopted us—no question! Scripture says that God gave six things to Israel—in the language of *The Message* translation: "They had everything going for them—family [the word is *adoption*], glory, covenants, revelation [receiving the law], worship, promises" (Romans 9:4).

Yes indeed, they had it all. What gifts God gave them! What grace He bestowed!

But someone says, "That's just the problem. The adoption and all these other gifts were given to the Israelites, not to us."

It appears so, doesn't it? But the next verses offer good news that excites our hearts. "For they are not all Israel who are of Israel, nor are they all children because they are the seed of Abraham; but, 'In Isaac your seed shall be called.' That is, those who are the children of the flesh, these are not the children of God; but the children of the promise are counted as the seed" (verses 6–8). This means that the adoption, the privilege of being a part of the royal family of God Himself, and all the other rich things that God gave to His people then belong to His people now. Those who have received Jesus Christ by faith are the children of Abraham by faith and the children of God by faith.

There is more. Much more. For Paul expanded this adoption thought—this being children of God thought; this actually being members of the heavenly family thought—with these additional words: "When the right time came, God sent his Son, born of a woman, subject to the law. God sent him to buy freedom for us who were slaves to the law, *so that he could adopt us as his very own children.* And because you Gentiles have become his children, God has sent the Spirit of his Son into your hearts, *and now you can call God your dear Father.* Now you are no longer a slave *but God's own child. And since you are his child, everything he has belongs to you"* (Galatians 4:4–7, NLT; emphasis added).

One of my favorite chapters is Ephesians 1. The first fourteen verses contain the phrase "in Christ" or its equivalent eleven times. In verse five comes the startling, delightful revelation that God has "predestined us to adoption as sons by Jesus Christ." Here's the genuine, glorious predestination that the Bible teaches: if you accept Jesus Christ, your adoption as a son or daughter of God is predestined. Fixed. Cut and dried. No question. You are a chosen child.

This predestination idea, this adoption idea, was conceived in the council of peace. The Father and the Son confirmed it with a handshake.[1] Jesus Himself fulfilled the thirty-three year contract. The adoption papers were signed at the cross, and they were sealed by His resurrection! So, there is absolutely no question about our being "chosen children." The only question is why He would adopt us in our condition.

2. God has adopted us despite our abhorrent condition. We can know what He saw in us by reading Romans 1:29–31: Human beings are "filled with all unrighteousness, sexual immorality, wickedness, covetousness, maliciousness; full of envy, murder, strife, deceit, evil-mindedness; they are whisperers, backbiters, haters of God, violent, proud, boasters, inventors of evil things, disobedient to parents, undiscerning, untrustworthy, unloving, unforgiving, unmerciful." Those who feel that this black list doesn't describe them should read Romans 3, which contains the following assertions: " 'There is none righteous, no, not one' " (verse 10); " 'There is none who does good, no, not one' " (verse 12); "All have sinned and fall short of the glory of God" (verse 23).

Talk about a dysfunctional family! The popular book of a couple decades ago entitled *I'm OK—You're OK* might better be retitled *I'm Dysfunctional—You're Dysfunctional.*

Dr. Petterson's family of origin might even be fairly normal compared to the family tree from which we sprouted. Every baby born on this planet since Adam and Eve is like a "crack baby." Our inheritance of evil is the worst imaginable. The environment out of which we come is at the lowest depths known to the wicked. As Paul says, "we are filled with all unrighteousness," lost, separated from God, cut off from heaven.

So why would God want to adopt us when we flip wads of chow mein on His royal lap and all we bowl is gutter balls? But He laid the plan anyway. He signed the adoption papers anyway. He chose us to be His children anyway. As the New Living Translation phrases Romans 5:8, "God showed his love for us by sending Christ to die while we were still sinners." A four-letter word is the only answer: *LOVE!*

3. God loves us as He loves His Son, Jesus. Is there assurance available for the believer?

> This is the lesson which Jesus taught while he was on earth, that the gift which God promises us, we must believe we do receive, and it is ours. . . .
>
> . . . Through this simple act of believing God, the Holy Spirit has begotten a new life in your heart. You are as a child [a chosen child] born into the family of God, and He loves you as He loves His Son.[2]

Remember the words that the Father spoke at the baptism of His Son? "Suddenly a voice came from heaven, saying, 'This is My beloved Son, in whom I am well pleased'" (Matthew 3:17). Ellen White said, "The word that was spoken to Jesus at the Jordan . . . embraces humanity. The voice which spoke to Jesus says to every believing soul, This is My beloved child [My chosen child], in whom I am well pleased."[3]

If I don't believe this, if I don't rejoice in this fact, if I don't revel in this assurance, if I don't take God at His word, would I not have an evil heart of unbelief?

My wife and I know a dear family who had two children of their own but who adopted two other children. Their final adoption was a little girl in Guatemala. We watched them agonize over the red tape, the seemingly ridiculous requirements, the snail-paced progress of the process. For two years they suffered the emotional highs and lows of thinking that things would work out and they would have their precious little one only to have their hopes dashed by some bureaucratic obstacle. We witnessed their persistence, their tenacity, and their love that captured and held them for that "eternity" because they had a little Guatemalan-girl-shaped vacuum in their hearts that could be filled when she was theirs.

"Long ago, even before He made the world, God loved us and chose us in Christ to be holy and without fault in His eyes. His unchanging plan has always been to adopt us into His own family. . . . And this gave Him great pleasure" (Ephesians 1:4, 5, NLT).

In his book *The Lost Boy*, Dave Pelzer wrote, "To be adopted is the highest honor bestowed on a child who longs to become a member of a family."[4] If Jesus is my Brother, and God is my Father, this makes me a member of the royal Family—a child of God. *A chosen child!* Is this not "blessed assurance"?

1. See Ellen G. White, *The Desire of Ages* (Nampa, Idaho: Pacific Press®, 1940), 834.

2. White, *Steps to Christ* (Hagerstown, Md.: Review and Herald®, 1956), 50, 52.

3. White, *The Desire of Ages,* 113.

4. Dave Pelzer, *The Lost Boy* (Deerfield Beach, Fla.: Health Communications Inc., 1997), 308.

CHAPTER 16

The Long, Steep Steps Syndrome

In his book *Empires in Collision,* Pastor George Vandeman told of a church in the city of Rome called Santa Maria d'Aracoeli.[1] An early Christian basilica, it was rebuilt by the Benedictines in the thirteenth century.

In 1348, a terrible plague struck the area and took many lives. The survivors wanted to make an offering to God to express their gratitude at being alive. So they built a marble stairway leading up to this sanctuary.

As Pastor Vandeman pointed out, their gift makes a striking picture of the human dilemma. The stairway has 122 steps. That's a lot of steps, and a long way to climb—and not exactly handicapped friendly.

To many people, the way to God seems as long and steep as those stairs. How do we climb up to the sanctuary of God? How can sinful human beings ever gain acceptance before a holy God?

The army says, "Be all that you can be." That's quite a stretch. But concerning salvation, God says, "Be all that Jesus was." That's an immeasurably greater stretch! It's tantamount to saying to people who find one flight of stairs challenging, "All you have to do to be saved is to climb Mount Everest." Or possibly, it is like the illustration I have often used. God is so high, so holy, so perfect, and we are such low, unholy, imperfect, spiritually flawed worms . . . so how in the world do we make it?

"It's simple," our spiritual guide says. "All you have to do is to jump across the Grand Canyon."

"But," we say, "that's miles across."

"I know. Just train for it."

"But Evel Knievel tried a smaller canyon once, and even on a motorcycle, he didn't begin to make it."

Our guide responds casually, "I know, but think positively. Just remember, God has only one requirement for making it to heaven: You just have to jump across the Grand Canyon, and you'll be safe forever!"

The syndrome illustrated

Ellen White described concerned sinners of the Dark Ages:

> Under the guidance of pope and priest, multitudes were vainly endeavoring to obtain pardon by afflicting their bodies for the sin of their souls. Taught to trust to their good works to save them, they were ever *looking to themselves*, their minds dwelling upon their sinful condition, seeing themselves exposed to the wrath of God, afflicting soul and body, yet finding no relief. . . . Thousands abandoned friends and kindred, and spent their lives in convent cells. By oft-repeated fasts and cruel scourgings, by midnight vigils, by prostration for weary hours upon the cold, damp stones of their dreary abode, by long pilgrimages, by humiliating penance and fearful torture, thousands vainly sought to obtain peace of conscience. Oppressed with a sense of sin, and haunted with the fear of God's avenging wrath, many suffered on, until exhausted nature gave way, and without one ray of light or hope they sank into the tomb.[2]

Such is the weight of self-dependence in climbing the long, steep steps in order to gain the favor of God.

Some time ago, a television program documented this same type of thinking. I watched as thousands of Hindus flocked to the Ganges River at Veranathi, a city four thousand years old. The river was brown with mud, and as I watched, dead animals floated by. And the ashes of some thirty thousand people a year cremated at this spot were sprinkled into the disease-laden waters. But Hindus regard these waters as sacred, and they believe they bring purity, wealth, and fertility to those who bathe in them.

In fact, millions believe the most sacred spot in the world is the place where the Ganges merges with the Jumna River. These people gather to immerse themselves in the waters, hoping that their sins will be carried away. They believe that those who die there are freed from endless reincarnations.

Righteous deeds, bodily mortifications, self-denials, Yoga, special knowledge, intense devotions . . . all these speak of the long, steep steps to heaven.

The flagellants in the Philippines are caught in the same sinister web. Perhaps you've seen the films. These people beat their bared backs with whips that have sharp pieces of metal bound into the cords. Soon, blood is running down their backs and soaking into their white trousers. Sometimes they become weak and fall, and, following their instructions, friends take their whips and beat them until they get up and struggle on to some designated church. They finish this gruesome torture by wading into the ocean and bathing in the salt water.

Why do they do this? They do it to reach perfection, to gain God's favor, to rack up merit so God will find them worthy and accept them.

This thinking cuts across all cultures. At certain stages of their lives, both Charles and John Wesley were trusting in themselves and their progress up the long, steep steps for their acceptance with God. Both of them faced near-death experiences without a genuine assurance of peace with God. A violent storm engulfed the ship on which John Wesley was traveling to America, and he feared for both his temporal and his eternal life. A group of German Moravians on board exhibited the calmness and trust that Wesley longed for. When he returned to England, he arrived at a clearer understanding of faith in Jesus Christ under the tutelage of a Moravian preacher. *The Great Controversy* recounts the story:

> At a meeting of the Moravian society in London a statement was read from Luther, describing the change which the Spirit of God works in the heart of the believer. As Wesley listened, faith was kindled in his soul. "I felt my heart strangely warmed," he said. "I felt I did trust in Christ, Christ alone, for salvation: *and an assurance was given me* [emphasis added], that He had taken away *my* sins, even *mine*, and saved *me* from the law of sin and death."
>
> Through long years of wearisome and comfortless striving—years of rigorous self-denial, of reproach and humiliation—Wesley had steadfastly adhered to his one purpose of seeking God. Now he had found Him; and he found that the grace which he had toiled to win by prayers and fasts, by almsdeeds and self-abnegation, was a gift, "without money and without price."[3]

The long, steep steps syndrome is perpetuated in the lives of many Seventh-day Adventist believers. They are earnest, sincere, striving, longing, struggling, and uncertain, lacking peace and assurance. The steps they're climbing look something like this: a compulsive focus on their performance, the "have tos," the commandments, "be ye therefore perfect," obedience, sanctification, holiness, and righteousness.

And it gets worse. Some seem to say, "When you never sin willfully; in fact, when you never sin, period; when you reflect the image of Jesus fully; when you've become all that Abraham was—and Job, Enoch, John the Baptist, Paul, and Ellen White and the rest of the pioneers combined; and when you are ready to live through the time of trouble without an intercessor; then—and then only—can you start to think about peace and confidence and the assurance of salvation."

How we live is important. But people who focus on the dos and don'ts as a main component of their spiritual life so often evidence a heaviness, an uncertainty, a gnawing, wondering, questioning about their present salvation. They seemingly have no time out from "the battle and the march"—precious little time for joy, peace, relief, praise, and rejoicing in the "Lamb of God who takes away the sin of the world."

The answers

The answers to the galling steep-steps syndrome are numerous. Finding the answers makes all the difference in the world to conscientious Christians who are sincerely concerned about "living up to the light," "following in the steps of Jesus," "keeping the commandments," "being an overcomer," "experiencing sanctification," "obedience," and "upholding the special counsels of Ellen White." And finding the answers doesn't make people any less faithful Seventh-day Adventists, but it does make them more Christian. Finding the answers doesn't make them less careful about the above-named concerns, but it does add a dimension of delight and joy and peace and assurance that they might previously have thought impossible. In fact, finding the answers may usher super-careful believers into an experience of fullness and relief and freedom that previously they might have looked upon, from the lofty heights of self-righteousness, with alarm, skepticism, and even outright hostility as being "cheap grace."

Before we propose some answers, let me endeavor to assure you of the direction we're taking by again posing a few questions and answers.

Doesn't the Bible teach that the nations of the saved who enter through the gates into the city are commandment keepers?

This is an indisputable fact.

When you accept Jesus Christ as your personal Savior, can you then go on sinning in the same abandoned fashion as before?

Paul gave the answer plainly in Romans 6:1, 2: "So what do we do?

Keep on sinning so God can keep on forgiving? I should hope not" *(The Message)*. Or, as the New Living Translation puts it, "Well then, should we keep on sinning so that God can show us more and more kindness and forgiveness? Of course not! Since we have died to sin, how can we continue to live in it?"

Are you leading us into "easy believism"?

Not even!

Aren't we beginning to teeter on the edge of "once saved, always saved"?

I cannot and do not entertain this unbiblical teaching!

Doesn't the Christian life include such things as overcoming, sanctification, and walking as Jesus walked?

Absolutely!

And now, let us hurry on to the answers to the long, steep steps syndrome. We must remember some very important cautions as we continue. Converted people do some very crummy things at times. Saints, believers, do actually sin. Christians perform or permit some very un-Christlike acts. The difference between the saint and the sinner is that saints hate the sin, confess it, and purpose not to repeat it, and, at a defining moment, achieve that goal; whereas sinners go on their merry way doing what comes naturally.

There is a definite difference between "falling into sin," or even choosing it, as a Christian, and the flagrant, abandoned lifestyle of following an open course of evil. This difference is recognized in this statement: "While the followers of Christ have sinned, they have not given themselves to the control of evil."[4]

Conversion doesn't mean that believers will no longer experience temptation or respond to evil or that the drives and propensities to sin are forever ended. Nor does it mean that they will never sin again. But it does mean that they know what to do and whom to turn to if sin rears its ugly head.

There is an element of truth in the bumper sticker that says, "Christians aren't perfect—just forgiven." The apostle Paul would have said "Amen" to this. However, he would also have hastened to add, "But I press on. . . . I press toward the goal for the prize of the upward call of God in Christ Jesus" (Philippians 3:12–14).

Sinning and asking forgiveness repeatedly is problematic. But there is a worse problem: Sinning and *not* asking for forgiveness. Sinning and feeling that you *can't ask* for forgiveness anymore. Sinning and *giving up*. Sinning and *forgetting* that we don't have to continue in that sin. Sinning and *staying away* from personal study and church worship.

We find the answer in the sanctuary services of long ago. When God's people became aware of sin in the life, they brought a "without spot or blemish" lamb to offer in their behalf at the sanctuary. God Himself had appointed this offering. It was a substitute offering—an "in place of"/ "instead of" offering. And when sinners placed their hands on the head of the lamb and confessed their sins, the lamb bore their sins. The lamb was slain in their place. A priest ministered the blood of the lamb in the presence of God, and the believers went away forgiven, pardoned, cleansed, joyful. The blood of the lamb made the sinning believers accepted . . . not with a "sinning license" but with a fresh, new determination to love and obey such a wonderful, loving, forgiving God.

The answer to how to get to heaven is to remember that our effort, sweat, blood, and tears can't get us there. Rather, Jesus said, *"I am the Way!"*

The answer to being at the wedding feast is to don the wedding garment provided by the King Himself—the gift of the King (see Matthew 22:3–12).

The answer to the righteous requirements of heaven is not "might and main," striving to *achieve* righteousness. The answer is to believe, receive, and accept what Jeremiah 33:16 heralds: "THE LORD OUR RIGHTEOUSNESS."

Jesus gave the answer when people asked Him, " 'What shall we *do*, that we may work the works of God?' " (John 6:28, emphasis added). Jesus said, " 'This is the work of God, that you may *believe* in Him whom He sent' " (verse 29; emphasis added).

The answer is what *The Desire of Ages* speaks of: *"The price of heaven is Jesus.* The way to heaven is through faith in the 'Lamb of God, who takes away the sin of the world.' "[5]

The answer is to find what Luther found while climbing Pilate's staircase on his knees—Jesus! It is to find what John Wesley found at the Moravian meeting—Jesus! To find what the paralytic found when he was let down through the roof—Jesus! To find what the thief found in the last few hours of his life—Jesus!

The answer is 1 John 1:9, "If we confess our sins, He is faithful and just to *forgive* us our sins and to *cleanse us from all unrighteousness*" (emphasis added).

The answer is 1 John 2:1, "My dear children, I am writing this to you so that you will not sin. But if you do sin, there is someone to plead for you before the Father. He is Jesus Christ, the one who pleases God completely" (NLT).

The answer is Colossians 2:10, "You are complete in Him."

The answer is, "When I try, I fail. When I trust, *He succeeds.*"

The answer is 1 Thessalonians 5:23, 24, which pictures God's will as being to "sanctify you *completely,*" meaning "your whole spirit, soul, and body" (emphasis added). Combine that with the marvelous promise in verse 24: "The One who called you is completely dependable. If he said it, *he'll do it!*" (*The Message;* emphasis added). The answer is that it's His work. His doing. It's my giving Him permission to do it.

The answer is that no matter how long we live, we're never one whit more righteous or holy or perfect than when we first accept Jesus Christ as our personal Savior. Oh, we will change, all right. We'll be different for sure. We'll grow into His likeness. We'll walk in the light. We'll fight the good fight of faith. But we won't do all of this to win salvation, for Christ has already won that for us. Rather, we'll do all of this because Christ leads us into it when we receive the gift of salvation that He bestows on us.

We can know

Wouldn't it be nice if a test could determine whether we are Christians—perhaps some kind of litmus paper that people could lick that would turn pink if they were and blue if they weren't? Or perhaps a spiritual X-ray device like we pass through at the airport. Maybe a spiritual lie-detector machine or some kind of computer analysis.

There *are* tests. We *can* know. There are enough comparisons, descriptions, and measurements so that we can be sure in spite of those who have come to feel that it is more spiritually "Hoyle" not to know and not to be sure. It seems Christ would tell those people, "You err, not knowing the Scriptures or the power of God."

Think about it. Here we are with the whole world coming apart, prophecies fulfilling every day right before our eyes, many of us believing the end of the world is imminent, and we're not supposed to know where we are spiritually? Whether or not we're Christians? Whether we're saved or lost at this moment? And this is God's will—this is the way it's supposed to be?

I mean, probation is about to close, and someone says, "Remember, uncertainty is the watchword," or "As long as you don't know whether or not you are saved, you're fine. But as soon as you find out, you're in trouble."

No!

No!

A relationship with Jesus Christ is measurable. Otherwise, the apostle John would not have been inspired to say, "I write to you who believe in the Son of God, so that you may *know* you have eternal life" (1 John 5:13, emphasis added).

The good news is that we can get off the long, steep steps mode of life.

The good news is that "the character is revealed, not by occasional good deeds and occasional misdeeds, but by the *tendency* of the habitual words and acts."[6]

The good news is that "we shall often have to bow down and weep at the feet of Jesus because of our shortcomings and mistakes [and sins], but we are not to be discouraged. Even if we are overcome by the enemy, we are not cast off, not forsaken and rejected by God."[7]

The good news is that I am justified by faith, sanctified by faith, and glorified by faith.

The good news is that we *can* be different than we are. We *can* overcome; we don't have to be "comer-overs." We *don't* have to sin. We *can* make it. We *can* be in heaven then and in heavenly places now—all because of what Jesus Christ became, the life He lived, the death He died, His resurrection, and His advocacy in the presence of the Father . . . *and all for us!*

Believers all need to ask themselves, "Who do I trust for my salvation, Jesus or me? His merits or mine? My pleasing the Father perfectly or His pleasing the Father perfectly in my behalf? The robe of righteousness that I have labored to weave with His help or the robe of righteousness without one thread of human devising? My overcoming or His? The work that I am doing or the work that Jesus did and is doing for me? Is my salvation based on my offering of my body as a living sacrifice or on His offering as the Lamb of God? On my sweat and blood or His bloody sweat?

If we are trusting in Jesus Christ for our present and eternal salvation, then in the midst of "the battle and the march," the striving, the struggle to yield our will, and the growing pains, we can feel the flood of relief, assurance, joy, thankfulness, and much praise. The reason? Because *in Christ* we are no longer consumed with and focusing on "the long, steep steps." Rather, our gracious Father looks upon us as standing on top of Mount Everest while we are still climbing!

---

1. George E. Vandeman, *Empires in Collision* (Nampa, Idaho: Pacific Press®, 1988), 17.

2. Ellen G. White, *The Great Controversy* (Nampa, Idaho: Pacific Press®, 1950), 72; emphasis added.

3. Ibid., 256

4. White, *Testimonies for the Church* (Nampa, Idaho: Pacific Press®, 1948), 5:474.

5. White, *The Desire of Ages* (Nampa, Idaho: Pacific Press®, 1940), 385; emphasis added.

6. White, *Steps to Christ* (Hagerstown, Md.: Review and Herald®, 1956), 57, 58; emphasis added.

7. Ibid., 64.

CHAPTER 17

Extreme Assurances and Promises

Now we've come to the last chapter. Some readers might be tempted to say, "There's an imbalance in your book. You didn't write enough about sin, standards, commandments, the 'battle and the march,' the striving, the 'work out your own salvation' part."

No! This book *is* the balance.

You see, we are a people of commandments, reforms, healthful living, Elijah types, new light, present truth, "give the trumpet a certain sound," "call sin by its right name," "we must be perfect and sinless so that after probation closes we can live without a Mediator." Our chief emphasis has been on doctrines, truths, and behavior. Even the special messenger to this church wrote, "As a people we have preached the law until we are as dry as the hills of Gilboa that had neither dew nor rain. *We must preach Christ in the law,* and there will be sap and nourishment in the preaching that will be as food to the famishing flock of God. We must not trust in our own merits at all, but in the merits of Jesus of Nazareth."[1]

Prior to this, she had expressed her heartfelt longing: "For years I have felt deep anguish of soul as the Lord has presented before me *the want in our churches of Jesus and His love.*"[2]

Undoubtedly, Seventh-day Adventists are a special people with a special message for these special end times. Indeed, we must give the trumpet a certain sound. At the same time, however, all of the teachings and doctrines and present truths must be bathed in the gospel, the beauty and simplicity of salvation, the rich assurances of righteousness by faith, and the grace-filled promises of life now, salvation now, as well as in the future.

The enemy of souls tempts some of us to focus on love, assurance, compassion, and relationship and to leave out the special messages for our times. But he pushes many of us into a cold formalism, harsh legalism, and gnawing uncertainty. He doesn't want us to combine our special truth with the beauty of love and assurance in Christ. This would be too powerful a package. It would be too winsome, too irresistible, too successful in bringing people to a final decision for Christ. So, he seeks an imbalance in which the people of God focus more on externals than internals. More on the law than on the gospel. More on miserable misgivings than on blessed assurances. He knows that all of this misrepresents the loving heart of the Father and repels rather than attracts and woos judgment-bound souls. That's why Ellen White wrote, "Satan is ready to steal away the blessed assurances of God. He desires to take *every glimmer of hope* and *every ray of light* from the soul; but you must not permit him to do this."[3]

The devil says, "Go ahead and preach your final messages, the law, health reform, high standards, and so forth, and don't get sidetracked with the simplicity of salvation, the beauty of salvation, the present assurance of salvation. After all, enough denominations out there already talk only about these. Just preach your 'present truth' and stay in your comfort zone of wondering and hoping, your miserable uncertainty about whether or not you are at this moment in a saving relationship to Christ."

Ellen White offered these insights:

> Satan is exultant when he can lead the children of God into unbelief and despondency. He delights to see us mistrusting God, doubting His willingness and power to save us. . . .
>
> Satan ever seeks to make the religious life one of gloom. He desires it to appear toilsome and difficult. . . .
>
> Many, walking along the path of life, dwell upon their mistakes and failures and disappointments, and their hearts are filled with grief and discouragement. . . .

. . . Let us group together the blessed *assurances* of His love, that we may look upon them continually.[4]

So, in this last chapter, I want to regale you with the promises and assurances of God, so that love will be the spring of action in your life, and your witness to this final generation will be winsome and fill the earth with the glory of God.

Scriptural assurances and promises

Read the following biblical passages again for the first time. Savor them.

> I will greatly rejoice in the LORD,
> My soul shall be joyful in my God;
> For He has clothed me with the garments of salvation,
> He has covered me with the robe of righteousness,
> As a bridegroom decks himself with ornaments,
> And as a bride adorns herself with her jewels (Isaiah 61:10).

" 'God so loved the world that He gave His only begotten Son, that whoever believes in Him should not perish but have everlasting life' " (John 3:16).

" 'He who believes in the Son *has* everlasting life' " (John 3:36, emphasis added).

" 'Most assuredly, I say to you, he who hears My word and believes in Him who sent Me *has* everlasting life, and shall not come into judgment, but *has* passed from death into life' " (John 5:24, emphasis added).

" 'This is the will of Him who sent Me, that everyone who sees the Son and believes in Him may have everlasting life; and I will raise him up at the last day' " (John 6:40).

" 'My sheep hear My voice, and I know them, and they follow Me. And I give them eternal life, and they shall never perish; neither shall anyone snatch them out of My hand' " (John 10:27, 28).

" 'This is eternal life, that they may know You, the only true God, and Jesus Christ whom You have sent' " (John 17:3).

"Much more then, having now been justified by His blood, we shall be saved from wrath through Him. For if when we were enemies we were reconciled to God through the death of His Son, much more, having been reconciled, we shall be saved by His life" (Romans 5:9, 10).

"To the praise of the glory of His grace, by which He *has made us accepted in the Beloved*" (Ephesians 1:6, emphasis added).

"By grace you *have been saved* through faith, and that not of your-selves; it *is the gift of God*" (Ephesians 2:8, emphasis added).

"In Christ Jesus you who once were far off have been brought near by the blood of Christ. Now, therefore, you are no longer strangers and foreigners, but fellow citizens with the saints and members of the household of God" (Ephesians 2:13, 19).

"I do not mean that I am already as God wants me to be. I have not yet reached that goal, but I continue trying to reach it and to make it mine. Christ wants me to do that, which is the reason he made me his. Brothers and sisters, I know that I have not yet reached that goal, but there is one thing I always do. Forgetting the past and straining toward what is ahead, I keep trying to reach the goal and get the prize for which God called me through Christ to the life above. All of us who are spiritually mature should think this way, too. And if there are things you do not agree with, God will make them clear to you" (Philippians 3:12–15, NCV).

"In Him dwells all the fullness of the Godhead bodily; *and you are complete in Him*" (Colossians 2: 9, 10, emphasis added).

"May God himself, the God who makes everything holy and whole, make you holy and whole, put you together—spirit, soul, and body—and keep you fit for the coming of our Master, Jesus Christ. The One who called you is completely dependable. *If he said it, he'll do it*" (1 Thessalonians 5:23, 24, *The Message;* emphasis added).

"By one offering He has perfected forever those who are being sanc-tified" (Hebrews 10:14).

"This is the testimony: that God has given us eternal life, and *this life is in His Son. He who has the Son has life;* he who does not have the Son of God does not have life. These things I have written to you who believe in the name of the Son of God, *that you may know that you have eternal life,* and that you may continue to believe in the name of the Son of God" (1 John 5:11–13).

How do you know if you really have the Son? " 'Behold, I stand at the door and knock. If anyone hears My voice and opens the door, *I will come in to him* and dine with him, and he with me' " (Revelation 3:20). If you've asked Jesus to come in, where is He? He's in your heart. This means you have the Son. This means that you *have* eternal life.

Should we not be encouraged? Should we not be assured? Should we not be full of thanksgiving and praise to our God? But there is more.

From the pen of Ellen G. White

" 'Jesus stands knocking, knocking at the door of your hearts, and yet, for all this, some say continually, "I cannot find Him." Why not? He says, "I stand here knocking." Why do you not open the door, and say, "Come in, dear Lord"? *I am so glad for these simple directions as to the way to find Jesus. If it were not for them, I should not know how to find Him whose presence I desire so much'* "(quoted in A. G. Daniells, *Christ Our Righteousness* [Hagerstown, Md.: Review and Herald®, 1941], 37; emphasis added).

"By the messengers of God are presented to us the righteousness of Christ, justification by faith, the exceeding great and precious promises of God's word, free access to the Father by Christ, the comfort of the Spirit, *the well-grounded assurance of eternal life in the kingdom of God*" (*Christ's Object Lessons* [Nampa, Idaho: Pacific Press®, 1941], 317; emphasis added).

"The acceptance of the Saviour brings a glow of perfect peace, perfect love, *perfect assurance*" (ibid., 420; emphasis added).

"In Christ their eternal life is *secure*" (*The Desire of Ages* [Nampa, Idaho: Pacific Press®, 1940], 356; emphasis added).

"It is when Christ is received as a personal Saviour that salvation comes to the soul" (ibid., 556).

Speaking of the thief on the cross: "It is His [Christ's] royal right to save unto the uttermost all who come unto God by Him" (ibid., 751).

"Our Saviour is not in Joseph's tomb. He has risen, and has proclaimed over the rent sepulchre, 'I am the resurrection and the life.' Let us show by our actions that we are living by faith in him. We can call upon him for assistance. He is at our right hand to help us. Each one of you may know for yourself that you have a living Saviour, that he is your helper and your God. *You need not stand where you say, 'I do not know whether I am saved.'* Do you believe in Christ as your personal Saviour? If you do, then rejoice" (*General Conference Bulletin,* April 10, 1901, 183; emphasis added).

"If you are right with God today, you are ready if Christ should come today" (*Last Day Events* [Nampa, Idaho: Pacific Press®, 1992], 74).

"The message from God to me for you is, 'Him that cometh to me I will in no wise cast out.' (John 6:37) If you have nothing else to plead before God but this one promise from your Lord and Saviour, you have the assurance that you will never, never be turned away. It may seem to you that you are hanging upon a single promise, but appropriate that one promise, and it will open to you the whole treasure house of the riches of the grace of Christ. *Cling to that promise and you are safe. Present this assurance to Jesus, and you are as safe as though inside the city of God*" (*Manuscript Releases,* vol. 10 [Silver Spring, Md.: Ellen G. White Estate, 1990], 175; emphasis added).

"There are many who have long desired and tried to obtain these blessing [of the covenant of grace] but have not received them, because they have cherished the idea that they could do something to make themselves worthy of them. . . . . Christ is our only hope of salvation. . . . In Him is our hope, our justification, our righteousness" (*Patriarchs and Prophets* [Nampa, Idaho: Pacific Press®, 1958], 431).

"We *need to know* and *may know* that Christ is abiding in our hearts by faith, and that we are abiding in Jesus by faith" (*Review and Herald®*, September 27, 1892; emphasis added).

"Those who know not what it is to have an experience in the things of God, who know not what it is to be justified by faith, who have not the witness of the Spirit that they are accepted of Jesus Christ, are in need of being born again" (ibid., May 12, 1896).

"Man is given the privilege of working with God in the saving of his own soul. He is to receive Christ as His personal Saviour and believe in Him. *Receiving and believing is his part of the contract*" (ibid., May 28, 1908; emphasis added).

"You cannot gain an entrance by penance nor by any works that you can do. No, God Himself has the honor of providing a way, and it is so complete, so perfect, that man cannot, by any works he may do, add to its perfection" (*Selected Messages,* book 1 [Hagerstown, Md.: Review and Herald®, 1958], 184).

"The human family are in trouble because of their transgression of the Father's law. But God does not leave the sinner until He shows the remedy for sin. The only-begotten Son of God has died that we might live. The Lord has accepted this sacrifice in our behalf, as our substitute and surety, on the condition that we receive Christ and believe on Him. The sinner must come in faith to Christ, take hold of His merits, lay his sins upon the Sin Bearer, and receive His pardon. It was for this cause that Christ came into the world. Thus the righteousness of Christ is imputed to the repenting, believing sinner. He becomes a member of the royal family, a child of the heavenly King, an heir of God, and joint heir with Christ" (ibid., 215).

"While we cannot claim perfection of the flesh, we may have Christian perfection of the soul. Through the sacrifice made in our behalf, sins may be perfectly forgiven. Our dependence is not in what man can do; it is in what God can do for man through Christ. When we surrender ourselves wholly to God, and fully believe, the blood of Christ cleanses from all sin. The conscience can be freed from condemnation. Through faith in His blood, all may be made perfect in Christ Jesus. Thank God that we are not dealing with impossibilities. We may claim sanctification. We may enjoy the favor of God. We are not to be anxious about what Christ and God think of us, but about what God thinks of Christ our Substitute. Ye are accepted in the Beloved" (*Selected Messages,* book 2 [Hagerstown, Md.: Review and Herald®, 1958], 32, 33).

"Our precious Savior has given His life for the sins of the world, and has pledged His word that He will save all who come to Him. 'God so loved the world, that he gave his only begotten Son, that whosoever believeth in him should not perish, but have everlasting life' (John 3:16). *These are the conditions of gaining eternal life. Comply with them, and your hope is secured, whether you live or die. Trust in the soul-saving Redeemer. Cast your helpless soul upon Him, and He will accept and bless and save you. Only believe. Receive Him with all your heart, and know that He wants you to win the crown of life. Let this be your greatest and most earnest request. Make an entire surrender, and He will cleanse you from every pollution, and make you vessels unto honor. You may be washed and made white in the blood of the Lamb. Thus you gain the victory. . . . In faith hold fast"* (ibid., 255; emphasis added).

"*We must know for ourselves,* by the evidence of God's Word, whether we are in the faith, going to heaven or not" (ibid., 382, 383; emphasis added).

"Christ has been loved by you, although your faith has sometimes been feeble and your prospects confused. But Jesus is your Saviour. He does not save you because you are perfect, but because you need Him and in your imperfection have trusted in Him. Jesus loves you, my precious child. You may sing, 'Under the shadow of Thy throne Still may we dwell secure; Sufficient is Thine arm alone, And our defense is sure' " (*Selected Messages,* book 3 [Hagerstown, Md.: 1980], 147).

"Christ looks at the spirit, and when He sees us carrying our burden with faith, His perfect holiness atones for our shortcomings. When we do our best, He becomes our righteousness" (ibid., 180).

"Look away from yourself. Do not think or talk of yourself. You cannot save yourself by any good work that you may do. The Lord Jesus has not made you a sin-bearer. He has not been able to find any human or angelic being to be a sin-bearer. . . . Think of the Saviour. Lay your sins, both of omission and of commission, upon the Sin-bearer. You know that you love the Lord; then do not worry away your life because Satan harasses you with his falsehoods. Believe that Jesus will and does pardon your transgression. He bore the sins of the whole world. He loves to have the weak and troubled soul come to Him and rely upon Him. Seek God in simple faith, saying, 'I believe; help thou mine unbelief.' The Lord does not readily cast off His erring children. He bears long with them.

His angels minister to every believing, trusting soul. Now, when you read these words, believe that the Lord accepts you just as you are, erring and sinful. He knows that you cannot blot out one sin; He knows that His precious blood, shed for the sinner, makes that one who is troubled, worried, and perplexed, a child of God" (ibid., 325).

"All that man can possibly do toward his own salvation *is to accept the invitation,* 'Whosoever will, let him take the water of life freely' " (*Seventh-day Adventist Bible Commentary,* vol. 6, ed. Francis D. Nichol [Hagerstown, Md.: Review and Herald®, 1957], 1071; emphasis added).

"Hanging upon the cross Christ *was* the gospel. . . . This is our message, our argument, our doctrine" (ibid., 1113).

"When probation ends, it will come suddenly, unexpectedly—at a time when we are least expecting it. *But we can have a clean record in heaven today, and know that God accepts us; and finally, if faithful, we shall be gathered into the kingdom of heaven"* (*Seventh-day Adventist Bible Commentary,* vol. 7, ed. Francis D. Nichol [Hagerstown, Md.: Review and Herald®, 1957], 989; emphasis added).

"In dying, *Jesus has made it impossible for those who believe on Him* to die eternally. . . . Christ lived and died as a man, that He might be God both of the living and of the dead. *It was to make it impossible to lose eternal life if they believe on Him"* (ibid., 926; emphasis added).

"Let not the destiny of your soul hang upon an uncertainty. *Know* that you are fully on the Lord's side" (*Testimonies for the Church* [Nampa, Idaho: Pacific Press®, 1948], 6:405; emphasis added).

Speaking to a minister: "Have you woven Christ into your character? *You need not be in uncertainty in this matter.* Has the Sun of Righteousness risen and been shining in your soul? *If so, you know it; and if you do not know whether* you are converted or not, never preach another discourse from the pulpit until you do" (*Testimonies to Ministers and Gospel Workers* [Nampa, Idaho: Pacific Press®, 1944], 440; emphasis added).

"As we seek to imitate Him, keeping our eye upon the mark of the prize, we can run this race with *certainty,* knowing that if we do the very best we can, we shall certainly secure the prize" (*Testimony Treasures* [Nampa, Idaho: Pacific Press®, 1949], 1:185; emphasis added).

"He presents us to the Father clothed in the white raiment of His own character. He pleads before God in our behalf, saying: I have taken the sinner's place. *Look not upon this wayward child, but look on Me*" (*Thoughts From the Mount of Blessing* [Nampa, Idaho: Pacific Press®, 1956], 9; emphasis added).

"God offered them, in His Son, the perfect righteousness of the law, . . . and thus through God's free gift *they would possess the righteousness* which the law requires" (ibid., 55; emphasis added).

"Know and believe the love that God has to us, *and you are secure;* that love is a fortress impregnable to all the delusions and assaults of Satan" (ibid., 119).

The present assurance of salvation

To be joyous and free in Christ, to be sure of our salvation through Christ, to have the assurance of acceptance, and the witness of the Spirit that we are indeed born again doesn't mean any of the following:

- We can sin with impunity.
- Light, truth, and obedience are of little weight.
- We're caught in the trap of "cheap grace" and "new theology."
- The standards of the law and the precious present truths of the Bible and the Spirit of Prophecy are irrelevant.
- We have fallen into the Adventist version of "once saved always saved."
- Sin is suddenly less sinful.
- We must downplay the three angels' messages.
- We are to minimize Seventh-day Adventist pillars and distinctives.

Rather, it means the following:

- In the midst of the battle and the striving, we will have calm and peace.

- We will experience a great sense of relief.
- Our testimonies will contain more praise and thanksgiving.
- Fear, depression, discouragement, and uncertainty won't characterize our relationship with Jesus Christ.
- Covered with the righteousness of Christ, we will be fitted for the time of trouble.
- When immersed in the assurance of salvation, the three angels' messages will be an attractive, compelling, winsome witness to the world.

I very much like the simple assurance of the man who listened to a popular radio preacher, Charles E. Fuller. The preacher had announced that the following Sunday he would be speaking on the subject of heaven. The following is a part of the letter written by this old man, who was very ill.

Next Sunday you are to talk about Heaven. I am interested in that land, because I have held a clear title to a bit of property there for over fifty-five years. I did not buy it. It was given to me without money and without price, but the Donor purchased it for me at tremendous sacrifice. I am not holding it for speculation since the title is not transferable. It is not a vacant lot.

For more than half a century I have been sending materials out of which the greatest Architect and Builder of the Universe has been building a home for me which will never need to be remodeled nor repaired because it will suit me perfectly, individually, and will never grow old. Termites can never undermine its foundations for they rest on the Rock of Ages. Fire cannot destroy it. Floods cannot wash it away. No locks nor bolts will ever be placed upon its doors, for no vicious person can ever enter that land where my dwelling stands, now almost completed and almost ready for me to enter in and abide in peace eternally without fear of being ejected.

There is a valley of deep shadow between the place where I live in California and that to which I shall journey in a very short time. I cannot reach my home in the City of Gold without passing through this dark valley of shadows. But I am not afraid because the best Friend I ever had went through the same valley long, long ago and drove away all its gloom.

He has stuck by me through thick and thin since we first became acquainted fifty-five years ago, and I hold His promise in printed form never to forsake me or leave me alone. He will be with me as I walk through the valley of shadows, and I shall not lose my way when He is with me.

I hope to hear your sermon on Heaven next Sunday from my home in Los Angeles, California, but I have no assurance that I shall be able to do so. My ticket to heaven has no date marked for the journey—no return coupon—and no permit for baggage.

Yes, I am all ready to go and I may not be here while you are talking next Sunday evening, but I shall meet you there some day.[5]

I covet and claim this kind of assurance, this kind of peace, this kind of readiness, through the amazing grace of our loving Lord Jesus Christ. And God means all who believe to have such assurance.

---

1. Ellen G. White, *Review and Herald®,* March 11, 1890; emphasis added.

2. White, *Testimonies for the Church* (Nampa, Idaho: Pacific Press®, 1948), 5:727; emphasis added.

3. White, *Steps to Christ* (Hagerstown, Md.: Review and Herald®, 1956), 53; emphasis added.

4. Ibid., 116, 118; emphasis added.

5. Paul Lee Tan, *Encyclopedia of 7,700 Illustrations* (Rockville, Md.: Assurance Publishers, 1979), 545.

Twenty-six Undeniable Spiritual Truths

In my journey toward the assurance of salvation I now enjoy, I have learned lessons, certain core beliefs have crystallized, and undeniable spiritual truths have shaped my joy, my peace, and my witness to those around me. I share these twenty-six truths with the hope that they will bless the hearts of others as they have blessed mine.

1. No matter the name—*Paul, Moses, Enoch,* no matter the good works, the extreme devotion, the level of sanctification the "saints" of the Bible might have appeared to have reached, no one will be in the kingdom but for God's amazing grace.

2. If I don't have salvation *now,* I don't have salvation at all. If I'm not ready for Christ to come *this moment,* I'm not ready at all.

3. I can have the joy, the peace and the assurance of salvation *right now,* without giving a smidgen of credence to the unscriptural "once saved, always saved" doctrine.

4. *Everything* in my spiritual life and growth comes *by faith.*

5. Every rich provision of God's grace and salvation *is a gift*—even faith itself!

6. If I'm planning to attend the wedding feast, the only way to dress for success is to accept and wear the garments the King has provided.

7. When you're visiting a person who is dying, you don't speak of the good news of the Old Testament sanctuary services, the 2,300 day/

year prophecy, or the mark of the beast. You just share the *good news of the gospel.*

8. The three angels' messages are much more than the *warning news* of the judgment, the fall of Babylon, and the danger in receiving the mark of the beast. These messages are laced with the *good news* of the gospel (Revelation 14:6) and the *good news* of righteousness by faith (verse 12).

9. The Laodicean message doesn't stop at Revelation 3:15–17, where we make Christ sick and are "wretched, miserable, poor, blind and naked." It ends with verses 18–21, *full of Jesus,* full of invitation, full of salvation, and full of overcoming power.

10. The summation of the Word of God is *Jesus. Jesus* plus nothing. *Jesus* first, last, best, only, and always! This eventuates in a Jesus-like life!

11. God is in the *saving* business, not the losing business. This means that if God has a shred of justification for saving me, He will.

12. In Philippians 3:13, Paul says, "I don't feel that I have already arrived" (CEV). In verse 14, he says his method of operation is to "run toward the goal." In verse 15, he writes, "All of us who are mature should think in this same way. And if any of you think differently, God will make it clear to you." If I have a blind spot, if I'm not up to speed on some point, and if I ask God to help me see this, *He will.*

13. I don't behave, perform, or obey to become sanctified. God sanctifies me (sets me apart) *so that* I behave, perform, and obey within His will.

14. Millions will be saved who keep Sunday, eat pork, and think the saved go to heaven immediately when they die. But they have believed Jesus, received Jesus, and are living up to the light they have.

15. It's hard to be lost. People have to resist and keep on resisting. They have to reject and keep on rejecting. They have to turn away and keep on turning away. They have to beat back the appeals of the Holy Spirit and keep on doing that. God has paid too big a price for them, and He isn't going to let them go easily. They'll have to work at it really hard.

16. "Be ye therefore perfect" (Matthew 5:48, KJV) is a heavy load, a discouraging goal, a great stumbling block for many conscientious souls. I find the fact that this verse comes in the setting of love helpful.

To me, the verse says, "Love like God loves." Luke 6:36, placed in exactly the same setting, says, "Be merciful, just as your Father also is merciful." Therefore, my prayer is, "Help me to love with Your kind of love, and let me show Your kind of mercy."

17. The greatest privilege in the world is to know Jesus Christ and to be a part of His end-time people.

18. A correct interpretation of Daniel 7:22 takes away the sting of the judgment, the fear of the judgment, the uncertainty of the judgment. All of the more accurate versions say something like "and a judgment was made *in favor of the saints.*" Praise God for our standing in the judgment *in Jesus Christ!*

19. The whole point of the Old Testament sanctuary's demonstration of the plan of salvation depended upon *bringing* a perfect offering, not on *being* a perfect offerer. The offering I present to God every day is " 'The Lamb of God who takes away the sin of the world!' " (John 1:29). He alone is the perfect, without-blemish Offering.

20. I am saved, not by my sinlessness, but by His. I am saved, not by my righteousness, but by His. I am saved, not by my merits, but by His.

21. When I try, I fail. When I trust, He succeeds!

22. The hymn doesn't say trust *or* obey. Our relationship with God isn't a matter of either "Commandment keeping, overcoming, living up to all the light you have" *or* "just believe, have faith, and peace." It is both. It is balance!

23. As someone said, "I am not what I want to be, and I am not what I'm going to be, but thank God, I'm not what I was."

24. Every Seventh-day Adventist Christian has both "liberal" and "conservative" beliefs, practices, and characteristics as far as someone else is concerned, so I want to be as hard on myself as I wish, but very easy on others. If I accept myself in Christ, then I want to do the same for others.

25. The Seventh-day Adventist Church has more light and more truth than any other church I know of. But if some other church has more light, more truth, and more Bible, I would wish to be a member of that church.

26. "The price of heaven is Jesus"! (Ellen G. White, *The Desire of Ages* [Mountain View, Calif.: Pacific Press®, 1940], 385.)

Jesus came "to seek and to save that which was lost," Luke 19:10, KJV.

For more about salvation in Christ, we recommend these books:

Searching for the God of Grace
Stuart Tyner

With a deeply hidden feeling of futility, many Christians try to take responsibility for their own salvation and blend it with Jesus' gift of atonement. Discouraged by their failures, they find no peace with God. In this book, Stuart Tyner examines the pages of history and biblical principles of God's character "to clear away a few more obstacles, burst a few more padlocks, and unbury the spectacular riches of God's grace."
Paperback, 304 pages.   978-0-8163-2152-0   0-8163-2152-3   US$17.99

Salvation 101—Christianity Made Simple
E. Lonnie Melashenko

Let's go right to the core of Christianity. In *Salvation 101—Christianity Made Simple,* Lonnie Melashenko explores the essentials of Christian faith, the bottom line of our religion. It's not all that complicated, but it can be hard to believe:

"Christ Jesus: Who, being in very nature God, did not consider equality with God something to be grasped, but made himself nothing, taking the very nature of a servant, being made in human likeness, And being found in appearance as a man, he humbled himself and became obedient to death—even death on a cross!" (Philippians 2:5–8, NIV).

Jesus paid it all. Come to Him and find faith, hope, and joy.
Paperback, 96 pages.   978-0-8163-2168-1   0-8163-2168-X   US$9.99

Order from your ABC by calling **1-800-765-6955,** or get online and shop our virtual store at **www.AdventistBookCenter.com.**
  • Read a chapter from your favorite book
  • Order online
  • Sign up for e-mail notices on new products

Prices subject to change without notice